THE QUIET CRUSADERS

THE QUIET CRUSADERS

*The Untold Story
Behind the
Minnesota Model*

DAMIAN MCELRATH, PH.D.

HAZELDEN
HP
PITTMAN
*Archives
Press*

HAZELDEN®

Hazelden
Center City, Minnesota 55012-0176

1-800-328-0094
1-651-213-4590 (Fax)
www.hazelden.org

Library of Congress Cataloging-in-Publication Data

McElrath, Damian.
     The quiet crusaders: the untold story behind the Minnesota model /
        Damian McElrath. p. cm.
     Includes bibliographical references.
     ISBN 1-56868-740-7 (paperback)
     1. Alcoholism—Treatment—Minnesota. 2. Drug abuse—
Treatment—Minnesota. 3. Alcoholism—Adjuvant treatment—
Minnesota. 4. Drug abuse—Adjuvant treatment—Minnesota.
I. Title.
     RC565.8.M6 M347 2001
     616.86'106'09776—dc21   2001024804

05 04 03 02 01   6 5 4 3 2 1

Cover design by David Spohn
Interior design by Ann Sudmeier
Typesetting by Stanton Publication Services

To Peter Butler, a friend of many years.

Contents

Introduction

This book looks at three men and their contributions to the field of chemical dependency during the 1960s, 1970s, and 1980s. A multifaceted disease, chemical dependency is characterized by physical, mental, and spiritual components. James West, M.D., made great strides in the physical treatment of chemical dependency. Robert Morse, M.D., increased our understanding of the mental component. Reverend Gordon Grimm addressed the spiritual dimension. Each of these men built upon a method of treatment known as the Minnesota Model.

The Evolution of Chemical Dependency Treatment

For a long time, wholistic treatment that embraced the trilateral components of chemical dependency eluded professionals who tried to treat alcoholism. Unable to grasp the roots and dimensions of the disease, those who treated it ended up locking drunks away in the psychiatric wards of mental institutions. This had been the standard practice for decades. With the birth of Alcoholics Anonymous (AA) in 1935, people began to learn how to treat the disease from a more wholistic perspective.

The roots of the Minnesota Model of treatment for chemical dependency have been wholistic from the outset. Yet over time that model has broadened its definition of wholistic, evolving from an approach that treats all aspects of the disease to an approach that looks at the whole person to treat needs both related to the disease and separate from it.

Three main tributaries contributed to the formation of the Minnesota Model: (1) the birth and growth of AA, (2) the evolution of a multidisciplinary treatment model at Willmar State Hospital beginning in 1950, and (3) the development of a program based on AA at Hazelden in an environment that responded to the dignity of each of the patients who arrived there.

AA had already established deep roots in Minnesota by 1950, when a psychiatrist named Nelson Bradley became superintendent of Willmar State Hospital, located in rural Minnesota about a hundred miles west of Minneapolis. Willmar was one of seven state "inebriate asylums"—the unenviable reference to treatment centers for alcoholism. The hospital also served mental patients, which reinforced the popular identification of alcoholism as a psychiatric problem. At that time, alcoholism was considered to be merely a symptom of a psychiatric condition.

Bradley, however, separated the alcoholics from the mentally ill and took the locks off the doors in the alcoholic wards—a very radical approach at that time. He began assembling a multidisciplinary treatment team, and, learning from the example of AA, in 1954 he convinced the State of Minnesota to create salaried positions for recovering alcoholics to work in state hospitals as counselors on alcoholism. These people became the heart and soul of the multidisciplinary team at Willmar. The other, nonrecovering professionals on the multidisciplinary team gained much from the counselors' insights and knowledge about alcoholism.

What emerged at Willmar were two concurrent levels of treatment and expertise. On one level, the recovering counselors educated the patients about the *nature* of the disease that gripped them: the physical compulsion, the mental obsession, and the spiritual self-centeredness. They shared with the patients their own powerlessness and how they discovered both a power greater than themselves and a set of spiritual exercises (the Twelve Steps) that they needed to practice to ensure their recovery. The second level of treatment belonged to the professionals—the physicians, psychiatrists, psychologists, and nurses—who concerned themselves with the *ef-*

fects of the illness as it impaired the alcoholics' mental, emotional, physical, social, and spiritual well-being.

But the differences between the nature of the disease and its effects were neither self-evident nor clearly defined, and it was not always apparent how these two levels of treatment could best fit together. The roles of the counselors and those, for example, of the psychologists in their dealings with the patients tended to intrude upon one another. Physicians were never quite sure about the nature of the physical compulsion of craving, and psychiatrists and psychologists were never clear about the mental obsession and the loss of control. It might have been easier for the clergy to understand the self-centeredness, given the human tendency to set one's own will (inordinate pride) against God's will (the role of religion), but the clergy person had not yet joined the multidisciplinary team in the early 1950s. At this time, the distinction between religion and the spiritual nature of the program remained obscure unless the clergy person was a recovering person. Moreover, it took some time for the professionals on the team, other than the recovering counselors, to grasp the full meaning of alcoholism as a primary disease— a disease in and of itself, rather than one resulting from another physical or psychological condition.

Like Bradley, Lynn Carroll, a recovering alcoholic who served as the first director of Hazelden, was determined to overcome the labeling of drunks as mentally ill. When Hazelden opened its doors in 1949, Carroll grappled with a central issue: Should he have some psychological or psychiatric background or training? He knew that there were a lot of problems that he "hadn't learned to work out quite right. And then I got to think—What the hell! I had had psychiatrists and psychologists and they didn't do me any good and I didn't know any other alcoholic that they ever did anything for."

Carroll concluded that since he was getting good results, he would continue doing what he did best. He developed a recovery course based strictly on the AA program and process. He was convinced that the only way an alcoholic could be helped was through the Twelve Steps and the sharing of stories with another alcoholic. All his lectures were related to the Steps of AA.

In the 1960s, under the direction of a nonrecovering psychologist named Dan Anderson, Hazelden adopted and began to refine the multidisciplinary approach that Bradley had started at Willmar. Both Willmar and Hazelden traversed some rough terrain on the path toward building smooth working relationships among the members of the multidisciplinary team.

For example, when Anderson arrived at Hazelden in 1961, he wanted to add the psychological profile of a patient (the Minnesota Multiphasic Personality Inventory) to the treatment process. Carroll considered this an insidious intrusion of psychological principles into the AA program. The counselors guarded against treating the disease of alcoholism as primarily a psychological disorder or the result of an underlying mental illness. They were reluctant to give too much, if any, weight to the findings of the Minnesota Multiphasic Personality Inventory (MMPI). Reading the "tea leaves" (the disparaging way that the counselors would refer to the results of the MMPI) provided no insight into the issue of powerlessness. It took the counselors awhile to become comfortable with the idea that the results of the test could point out certain growth areas that the patient could pursue to support continuing sobriety. For example, assistance in dealing with a patient's predisposition toward anger and its inappropriate expression would also benefit a person's long-term sobriety.

Likewise, the professionals were sometimes skeptical of the AA program components. At Willmar, for example, after seeing schizophrenia in the MMPI results of a patient, Anderson commented to Fred Eiden, a recovering counselor, "Fred, this one's a real sick one."

Eiden would say something like, "I don't know, Dan, he seems to be getting the program." For Anderson, who was just starting his career, Eiden's response was meaningless. He remembered thinking, "When one is that disturbed, what did it mean 'to get the program'? And who would win out? Fred would win if this crazy guy remained sober."

Anderson recalled another situation: "I would see a guy who was well, I tested him, and I said to Fred, 'Fred, he's in good shape—not crazy—intelligent, and should be a great surgeon someday' (or something to that effect). Fred would say, 'He doesn't have the program though, Dan.'"

Gradually, the counselors, psychologists, and psychiatrists built enough trust to learn from each other. What evolved at Hazelden under Anderson was a treatment model that dealt with all aspects of the disease of chemical dependency. Now replicated throughout the world, this Minnesota Model taps into the success of AA in three ways:

1. It depicts alcoholism as a physical-mental-spiritual illness.
2. It follows the Twelve Steps, which outline the problem, the solution, and the spiritual exercises needed to follow the solution.
3. It promotes the AA Fellowship, wherein recovery takes place with one alcoholic talking informally to another, most often over a cup of coffee, putting into practice the human and spiritual principles of dialogue and identification.

A Wholistic View of Chemical Dependency

The wholistic description of alcoholism as a mental, physical, and spiritual illness is found in the Big Book: ". . . for we have been not only mentally and physically ill, we have been spiritually sick."[1] The spiritual dimension stems from the self-centered orientation of alcoholics. Preoccupied with their own wants, alcoholics exclude and disregard others. "When the spiritual malady is overcome, we straighten out mentally and physically."[2]

The Swiss psychiatrist Carl G. Jung touched on the spiritual dimension of wholeness in a letter to Bill W dated January 30, 1961: "His (Roland H's) craving for alcohol was the equivalent, on a low level, of the spiritual thirst of our being for wholeness, expressed in medieval language: the union with God." In this context, our yearning for *wholeness* is a yearning for *holiness*. Both words have the same root.

Alcoholism is a spiritual, unwholesome, unholy illness because it tears apart and rends asunder an individual's relationships with oneself, with one's family and others, and with one's Higher Power. Self-centeredness destroys the circle of relationships. Conversely, a wholistic approach to the treatment of the illness seeks to repair and set the individual back into those relationships and restore the circle, the signature symbol of wholeness.

The mental aspect of alcoholism is the mind's dominating obsession with the need to control one's drinking. This unfulfilled goal gives rise to the "insanity" (in reality a lack of wholeness or completeness) mentioned in the Second Step. Each time alcoholics take a drink they truly believe, contrary to all past experiences, that this time will be different, that they will control or moderate the number of drinks they will consume. This insanity, this obsession, this mental dimension of the illness is quite distinct from other psychiatric disorders and should not be confused with them.

As a physical illness the key characteristic is the compulsion, the craving to continue to drink once the first ounce has been imbibed. "At a certain point in the drinking of every alcoholic, he passes into a state where the most powerful desire to stop drinking is of absolutely no avail. This tragic situation has already arrived in practically every case long before it is even suspected."[3] In the Big Book this physical craving is compared to an allergy, though that analogy is no longer scientifically tenable.

To treat the whole person in the context of this definition of alcoholism is to deal with the physical, mental, and spiritual dimensions of the illness. This is what AA sought to do with the Twelve Steps and the Fellowship meetings, during which one alcoholic would talk with another over a cup of coffee.

Bradley made a great contribution to the progression of treatment when, as a nonrecovering person, he recognized and convinced others that recovering people possessed rare insight into the nature of the disease and that they had great success in helping their own. ("But the ex-problem drinker who has found this solution, who is properly armed with facts about himself, can generally win the entire confidence of another alcoholic in a few hours. Until such an understanding is reached, little or nothing can be accomplished."[4]) The firsthand experience that recovering counselors offered was essential to the success of the multidisciplinary team.

Improving the Minnesota Model

The three individuals portrayed in this book each worked with the Minnesota Model but also took it a step further, adding important developments to the treatment process. The men represent three

renowned programs: James West was instrumental in developing
the Betty Ford Center in Rancho Mirage, California, which is now
in its twentieth year; Robert Morse established the Mayo Addiction
Services in Rochester, Minnesota, nearly thirty years ago; and
Gordon Grimm spent thirty years in Center City, Minnesota, at
Hazelden, which recently celebrated its fiftieth anniversary.

James West gained much wisdom and knowledge from his personal recovery and from his professional experience as a physician
treating chemically dependent people in Chicago for thirty years.
When the Betty Ford Center opened in 1982, West brought not
only his many years of experience, but also an in-depth knowledge
of a variety of detoxication models. West contributed to the Minnesota Model by defining the partnership of the physician on the
multidisciplinary team. He was intent on educating medical students and other physicians in the nature and treatment of chemical
dependency and set up the Professionals in Residence Program at
the Ford Center. By including the physician in the treatment planning of every patient, West increased the Minnesota Model's ability
to treat the physical dimensions of wholeness.

Robert Morse increased the Minnesota Model's ability to treat
the mental dimensions of wholeness. In the 1960s most psychiatrists still regarded alcoholism as a secondary illness, resulting from
some other condition. After starting the Mayo Addiction Services
(initially called the Alcohol and Drug Dependency Unit) in 1972,
Morse quickly discovered that "crazy" behavior did not always dis-
appear when patients began to recover from chemical dependency.
This understanding, along with his medical and psychiatric training, enabled Morse to provide a model of treament at the Mayo
Clinic that acknowledged patients with the dual diagnosis of chemical dependency and other mental health problems. Morse is cred-
ited with "medicalizing" the Minnesota Model because he was able
to treat other medical conditions while patients were in rehabilitation. Like other programs at Mayo, the Addiction Services also contributes research to the advancement of knowledge in the field, and
it provides educational opportunities for medical students and
young physicians.

Both Morse and West built upon what Bill W clearly recognized when he wrote in the Big Book: "But this does not mean that we disregard human health measures. God has abundantly supplied this world with fine doctors, psychologists, and practitioners of various kinds. Do not hesitate to take your health problems to such persons. Most of them give freely of themselves, that their fellows may enjoy sound minds and bodies. Try to remember that though God has wrought miracles among us, we should never belittle a good doctor or psychiatrist. Their services are often indispensable in treating a newcomer and in following his case afterward."[5]

At Hazelden starting in 1965, Grimm defined the role of the chaplain who ministers to patients afflicted with the illness of chemical dependency. After years of wrestling with the nature of the chaplain's position, Grimm came to understand the illness as a deeply spiritual one, yet independent of a person's religious persuasion or lack thereof. In 1966 he instituted Hazelden's Clinical Pastoral Education Program, whose graduates have greatly increased our understanding of the spiritual dimension of chemical dependency. Grimm insisted that the chaplains at Hazelden be placed on the same plane as other professionals, rather than in the subsidiary roles that they experienced in other institutional settings. They were actively involved in the multidisciplinary team, the Fellowship, the relational dimensions of the Twelve Steps, and the caring community concept. By defining the role of the clergy, Grimm developed the Minnesota Model's spiritual dimension of wholeness.

Notes

1. *Alcoholics Anonymous,* 3d ed. (New York: Alcoholics Anonymous World Services, 1976), 64.
2. Ibid.
3. Ibid., 24.
4. Ibid., 18.
5. Ibid., 133.

THE QUIET CRUSADERS

Courtesy James W. West

James W. West, M.D.
Alcoholism—An Illness of the Body

James West was one of those rare doctors whom the alcoholic and the chemically dependent could look to for understanding and assistance. It was common knowledge that all too often physicians did not take adequate histories, did not identify chemical dependency as a medical problem, and did not involve themselves in making treatment recommendations or referrals for alcoholism and other drug dependencies. West was aware that medical school curricula virtually disregarded problem drinking. Yet since the 1960s, those who have worked with the Minnesota Model of treatment have recognized that the best way to help nonaddicted people understand the process of recovery is for them to see it happen. When involved in the recovery process in a peer setting, these adults experience a profound change of attitude about people afflicted with the illness of chemical dependency. After observing recovery firsthand, the nonaddicted no longer view chemical dependency as a moral issue or a question of willpower.

West possessed a rare ability not only to reach the afflicted but also to help others understand the afflicted. As medical director of the Betty Ford Center in Rancho Mirage, California, West established chemical dependency training programs for medical students and for physicians and other professionals. He also expanded the Minnesota Model to include physicians in treatment planning, thereby defining their role on the multidisciplinary team.

Early Life and Education

James W. West was born in Chicago on March 29, 1914. His father, Raymond Hall West, was English and his mother, Eleanor Ward, Irish. He was very fond of his three wonderful sisters, Mary Rose, Elinor, and Catherine Ann. The family moved to Oak Park, Illinois, when he was a young boy, and he attended grammar school at St. Lucy's, in neighboring Austin.

In elementary school he was full of mischief. He and his closest friend, Bayard Molder, had a reputation as young troublemakers, capable of disrupting the class at any time. West remembers one time when the two of them came in late for class. The nun who taught the class eyed them suspiciously and then ordered them to empty their pockets on the desk. She soon regretted her command, but all she could do was shout at them for the mess that they were making when they strewed greasy automobile parts on her immaculate and orderly desk. (Decades later, when West was visiting a nun who had been a recent surgical patient, he met his former St. Lucy's principal. He had a difficult time keeping a serious demeanor when she began introducing him to the other sisters in the nursing home and proclaiming him to be one of the best-behaved students that she ever had.)

After the boys completed the fifth grade, their parents were advised that the two of them should not remain in the same school as they would probably continue to aid and abet one another in their mischief making. The sisters at St. Lucy's heaved a collective sigh of relief when West's parents transferred him to the grammar school on the Notre Dame campus in South Bend, Indiana, for grades six through eight. The mission of the school was to provide "a total education for Catholic gentlemen." His recollections of the school's mission are hazy, but he remembers well the Notre Dame football team that practiced a short distance from his school. It was the era of the famous "four horsemen"—Edgar (Rip) Miller, Elmer (The Thin Man) Layden, Jim (Sleepy Jim) Crowley, and Harry (Stuly) Stuhldreher—who occasionally chatted with their young admirers.

When West finished grammar school, he chose to go to high

school at Campion Hall, a Jesuit boarding school in Prairie du Chien, Wisconsin. Recruiters for the school influenced his decision, but he later realized what a wise choice he had made because of the excellent education he received there. While making a retreat during his junior year at Campion he decided that he would dedicate his life to helping other people as a doctor. By the time he left Campion he was already a doctor in his mind. His conviction was so strong that he went through his subsequent education and all the credentialing required without the least bit of difficulty.

West began premedical studies at Loyola University in Chicago in 1932. During his first year, he met his future wife, Shirley Jane Crews. A junior in high school, she was popular, elegant, and attractive. West wondered about his chances among her many admirers, but he didn't need to worry; they were married on June 25, 1938.

While at Loyola, West decided to become a surgeon, yet he continued to exercise his passion for boxing. When he broke his hand while boxing for the Oak Park YMCA, he finally realized that the sport was incompatible with his vocation; he needed his hands for more serious goals than proving his athletic abilities in the ring. West continued his medical studies at Loyola, graduating in 1940.

In 1941 West began an internship and an eighteen-month preceptorial in surgery at Cook County Hospital in Chicago, which qualified him for the American Council of Surgeons. He was an associate attending surgeon at Cook County Hospital and an assistant clinical professor of surgery at Loyola University School of Medicine from 1949 until 1965. Early in his career, at the Little Company of Mary Hospital in 1950, he was an important member of the surgical team that performed the first kidney transplant in the world. Later, from 1965 until 1981, he helped establish a residency in surgery at this hospital.

From 1955 until 1965 West studied psychiatry and wrote a number of papers on drug and alcohol addiction, for which he obtained an associate membership in the American Psychiatric Association. The articles attracted attention at Rush-Presbyterian-St. Luke's Medical Center, where he later became an assistant professor in the department of psychiatry.

Recovery

West's own personal encounter with the effects of alcoholism was probably the major reason he became increasingly involved in the field of chemical dependency as his career progressed. In those early years from 1941 until 1945 he developed a very successful practice. But he also had a taste for alcohol, which gradually evolved into sporadic binge drinking, diagnosed as periodic alcoholism.

When he drank too much he had the good sense to stay away from the hospital. His wife was concerned but was uncertain what was happening with him. By chance she came across an article on AA in the *Saturday Evening Post*. She asked her husband to call AA, but he procrastinated. Eventually, she herself called, and on June 15, 1945, two recovering men from AA came to call on him. That became his first sobriety date; he remained abstinent and faithfully attended AA meetings until 1950. During those first five years, however, he was more interested in protecting his surgical career than in using the principles and practice of AA to achieve permanent sobriety. From 1950 until 1958 he drank three times; after the third slip he finally "got it," namely, that he had a disease and had to deal with it accordingly. It was no longer simply a question of protecting his career.

Chicago Practice

During those first thirteen years in recovery, he was looked upon as "the young doctor in AA" and was very generous with his time and efforts in helping other alcoholics. Patients came to him because they trusted that he could identify what their needs were. At first he would bring them to the Detox Center at Martha Washington Hospital in Chicago, which was about the only treatment available. After he heard about the opening of Hazelden in 1949, he and other AA members would bring patients there by train on the Old Milwaukee Road. He would stay for a day or two and either listen to a lecture by Lynn Carroll, the director of Hazelden, or he himself would give a talk at Carroll's request. He recalls that Carroll was inspirational when he talked about the Steps and their important role in recovery. Occasionally when West returned, Carroll would be lecturing on the same Step that West had heard previously, and he would marvel that Carroll had not changed a word.

West began bringing alcoholic patients to Lutheran General Hospital in 1960, when Nelson Bradley moved from Willmar State Hospital in Minnesota to Lutheran General to replicate the Minnesota Model of treatment in Chicago. West sent priests to Guest House in Lake Orion, Michigan, which had opened in 1952. When the Alcohol and Drug Dependency Unit at Mayo opened in 1972 under the direction of Robert Morse, West referred physicians to Mayo. It was much easier to send doctors to Mayo rather than to Hazelden. They would then be able to tell the curious and those who did not need to know that they were at Mayo to have a physical checkup, without revealing that it was being done at the chemical dependency clinic.

Helping Priests and Nuns

West first met Monsignor Ignatius McDermott of the Archdiocese of Chicago in 1948. The two developed a singular friendship with a shared concern for alcoholics. McDermott was in the habit of telephoning West whenever he had a priest who needed help. West would put the priest in the hospital with another diagnosis (usually gastroenteritis), detox the priest, and upon discharge refer him to AA. Often he himself would accompany the reluctant first-timer. Many times, however, that was not enough, and the priest without any continuing care would most likely fall back into his former drinking patterns.

A breakthrough occurred when John Patrick Cardinal Cody, the archbishop of Chicago, invited McDermott and West to his residence in 1965 to develop a plan to assist the priests and nuns within his archdiocese. The two agreed to help and suggested that the first order of business would be to call a general educational conference for the religious staff about issues related to the disease of chemical dependency and the need for intervention and rehabilitation. The turnout was very large, filling the auditorium at Holy Name Cathedral. Shortly after that, West sent the first nun from the archdiocese to Hazelden. She raised many an eyebrow on the unit and throughout the corridors because she would not be persuaded to shed her habit and dress in ordinary lay clothes. But she shortly became a cherished and cooperative client and completed treatment to the genuine applause of both patients and staff.

McDermott and West spent some time educating Cardinal Cody about the nature of alcoholism and the need to treat those who were chemically dependent like any other employee in the diocese who came down with another illness. Those who were chemically dependent had to be relieved of their duties temporarily to receive treatment. If they recovered and returned to their duties, they would still maintain their seniority for promotion. Before West would intervene on anyone, the concerned parties had to provide concrete and specific data that alcohol or chemicals were having a deleterious effect on the life of the person in question.

When McDermott called with the required data, West would visit with the candidate, most often at the church rectory. He was accustomed to being greeted in a variety of ways: sometimes the housekeeper had been told to tell him that the priest was not at home; sometimes a priest would simply deny that he had a problem; or he might dress West down for confronting him in his own home. Whatever the reception, West got right down to business and told him that arrangements had already been made to put him on disability leave. Usually the priest was on his way the very next day to Guest House in Michigan. As part of the aftercare program, the priests returning from treatment were obliged to attend conferences conducted by two psychologists, one of whom was a priest. On average, eight of every ten priests stopped drinking, changed their behavior, and were able to resume their pastoral duties. McDermott and West were considered so successful that Cardinal Cody sought them out to solve other problems unrelated to chemical dependency.

Recovery in a Hospital Setting

West became even more active on behalf of alcoholics in 1972 when he convinced the sisters of the Little Company of Mary, a general hospital in Evergreen Park, Illinois, that, since alcoholism was a disease and hospitals were the places where diseases were treated, the nuns should put in a program for alcoholics. Hospitals were still reluctant to admit alcoholics under any diagnosis, both because of their disruptive behavior and because they rarely paid their bills. West, however, presented the example of St. Thomas Hospital in Akron, Ohio. In 1939 Dr. Bob, one of the cofounders of AA, had talked to one of the staff nuns there about alcoholics: "Sister, these people need medical treatment—*I know.* Do you think we could smuggle at least a couple who I'm sure I could help in here." She agreed, and the two of them would bootleg the alcoholics into St. Thomas under the diagnosis of acute gastritis. "To prevent discovery of their deception, they ensconced the patients who were in the most acute stages of withdrawal in the hospital's 'flower room'—a nook previously used only for patients who had died and were awaiting removal to the morgue or funeral parlor."[1]

The hospital administrator at the Little Company of Mary was convinced, and West started a program for alcoholics. For three months, West trained the nurses and interns in how to assess the symptoms of alcoholism beyond the most visible, that of intoxication. It was a very simple program. The protocols for detoxication were initiated in the emergency room, the usual point of entry for alcoholics, who were then transferred to an empty bed on most any floor of the hospital. No special ward or "flower room" was set aside for them. For the remainder of their stay their treatment consisted of being taken or wheeled to lectures and to group services directed by a counselor. These patients also attended AA meetings that were scheduled at the hospital in the evenings.

West viewed the general hospital program not as short-term treatment but rather as the entry point to long-term treatment, either as an outpatient with AA involvement and professional counseling or as an inpatient in one of the alcoholism rehabilitation centers. He also believed that the program could easily be adapted to other general hospitals, without necessarily replicating all of the components at the Little Company of Mary. For example, some of the more elaborate psychosocial group therapeutics would not be necessary for all general hospital programs. Local AA volunteers from the community could provide much good counseling, and many hospitals already had AA groups that met in a room at the hospital.

Haymarket—Social Detox

At Little Company of Mary, West became an expert on detoxication practices. He expanded this knowledge even further at Haymarket House, which he founded jointly with McDermott on New Year's Eve in 1975. The ultimate goal of the two men was to bring about a radical change in the public perception of alcoholism.

In 1974 West had noted that the education of professionals and the community at large had helped immensely in raising people's

Monsignor Ignatius McDermott of the Archdiocese of Chicago and Dr. James West. These two founded the Haymarket House in Chicago on New Year's Eve in 1975. Courtesy James W. West

awareness of alcoholism as an illness just like any other illness, for which the best possible treatment should be provided. West perceptively outlined the factors that were raising the nation's social consciousness of chemical dependency:[2]

1. The legal factor, the Uniform Practice Act, which removed the inebriates from the criminal justice system.
2. The "green power," or money from the federal government for the treatment of alcoholism and for the training of health care professionals.
3. The insurance coverage (more green power) mandated state by state to cover treatment for chemical dependency.

At Haymarket, West put into practice a new form of substance-abuse treatment—social setting, or ambulatory, detox, which allowed for detoxication to take place in any social setting—that is, away from the more expensive setting of a hospital and without the use of drugs. Patients were free to walk around, since they were not confined to a hospital ward. A nonmedical person was trained to watch patients and to check pulse rates and blood pressure. Detoxication

The Haymarket House in Chicago, founded by Monsignor Ignatius McDermott and Dr. James West in 1975. The Haymarket House implemented a nonhospital, nondrug detoxication model—a Social Setting Detoxication Center.

generally took twenty-four to forty-eight hours, depending on the chemical ingested.

While the function of social setting detoxication is limited, the principle is sound and the reach widespread. Detox drugs are not necessary in a social setting and with low-level acute alcoholism. The effectiveness of Haymarket and the treatment of its clients "must be judged on its ability to detoxify clients, not on its ability to rehabilitate, which is an altogether different function not suited to the purpose of a detoxication facility. . . . The Social Setting Detoxication Center [is] an effective part of the alcoholism treatment network, [acting] as an entry point into long term care for an appreciable percentage of previously 'hopeless' and homeless persons."[3]

Other Efforts to Help Alcoholics

Besides Haymarket and the Little Company of Mary program, West was engaged in other activities on behalf of the chemically dependent. In 1974 he became assistant professor in the department of psychiatry at Rush-Presbyterian-St. Luke's hospital and a lecturer in the department of psychiatry at the University of Chicago. He was able to distinguish clearly for his audiences the roles that psychiatry could and could not play in helping the chemically dependent.

When the State of Illinois was developing a state-of-the-art program for credentialing chemical dependency counselors, West shared his extensive experience and expertise to help define the requirements for state licensure.

Up until 1973 West had been helping physicians on a personal, informal basis, particularly when they came to him for help. In order to expand this assistance in a more formal way, West founded and chaired the Impaired Physicians Committee of the Illinois Medical Society in 1975. To represent the various districts in the State of Illinois, he selected a group of between 15 and 20 doctors to serve as resources (and, when needed, as interventionists) for doctors and their families. The committee sent a mailing to the private home of each physician explaining how its representatives could provide help to those doctors who needed it, offering an assessment process and treatment options. From his own personal experience,

West was counting on the fact that many of the wives of the physicians would be curious enough to open and peruse the materials.

West also participated on boards and committees of various addiction societies in Illinois, one of which was by appointment of the governor. His background and experience made him the perfect match for the Betty Ford Center, the next stage of his journey in helping the addicted.

Eisenhower Medical Center Outpatient Program

In 1973 West gave a talk entitled "Alcoholism in a General Hospital" to a convention of physicians gathered at the Breakers' Hotel in Palm Beach, Florida. In the audience listening to the presentation were Joe Cruse and Paul Ohliger, who had been thinking about installing an alcohol program at their hospital facility, the Eisenhower Medical Center in Rancho Mirage, California. That evening over dinner, the three shared their visions of helping alcoholics in a hospital setting. It was the beginning of a professional relationship that eventually led to West's appointment as medical director of the Betty Ford Center at the Eisenhower Medical Center.

In the years following their dinner conversation, Cruse kept in touch with West, who spent winters in Palm Springs, just fifteen miles west of Rancho Mirage. In the meantime, Cruse was developing an outpatient program, which opened in 1978 at the Eisenhower Medical Center. When West retired from surgical practice at the end of 1981, he relocated permanently in Palm Springs, and Cruse asked him to assume the job of medical director of the outpatient program.

West was quick to accept this opportunity to continue his work with the chemically dependent. Pairing up with Helen Lightner Smith, a nurse and the liaison between the medical center and the outpatient program, West and Smith provided a series of in-service seminars for the hospital nurses on alcoholism and its symptoms. The nurses learned how to work with the physicians and patients to suggest, with sensitivity and diplomacy, that the patients they identified might need further help. They then pointed to the availability of the outpatient program. West wrote up the standing orders for detoxication, which included calling the outpatient program. In the course of a few months, the census for the outpatient program increased from five patients to thirty.

The Betty Ford Center

West met former first lady Betty Ford through Cruse, who had been Ford's personal physician. As recovered alcoholics themselves, all three of them shared an interest in building programs to help those affected by chemical dependency. Cruse inspired Ford to found a treatment center, and she reluctantly agreed to have it bear her name.

As the preparations evolved for the opening of the Betty Ford Center, West became an essential member of the planning team. In August and September before the October 4, 1982, opening, Cruse would invite West and John Schwarzlose (then clinical manager and later president of the Betty Ford Center) to his home, where, after a long day of meetings and training, the three of them would relax in the jacuzzi while recounting the successes and failures of the day and wondering with all the work that still remained whether it would all be done in time. Somehow, they managed to put everything in place by the scheduled opening day.

As the center's first medical director, Cruse estimated that about 25 percent of the patients would have to be detoxed using the expensive hospital facilities at the Eisenhower Medical Center. But West's knowledge of ambulatory and social detox and the medications that he employed to abort the symptoms of withdrawal meant that very few patients had to be transferred to Eisenhower for more intensive monitoring. Ambulatory detoxication turned out to be the ideal practice for the Betty Ford Center, which had just received the newly written and recently promulgated license from the State of California for a chemical dependency recovery center located outside of a hospital setting.

With West's extensive experience in treating alcoholics and other chemically dependent people, the medical component of the Betty Ford Center became one of its great strengths. When he became the medical director of the center in 1984, West assumed full responsibility for the medical component of the rehabilitation program and became an active member of the multidisciplinary treatment team.

As part of each individual treatment plan, West made sure that all patients received excellent medical care. He believed that he was responsible for the physical well being of every patient in the Betty Ford Center; every patient admitted to the center was to have a complete physical and follow-up. By including the physician in the treatment planning of every patient, West defined the role of the physician on the multidisciplinary team.

West was a superior lecturer. While medical director he was accustomed to presenting three lectures every month, a synopsis of the material that he once gave to the medical students whom he taught. He provided patients with information about the psychosocial signs and symptoms of alcoholism and drug addiction; about the pharmacology of addictive diseases, cross addiction; and about the medical consequences of alcoholism. He had the knack of translating some of the more difficult material into language comprehensible and stimulating to the patients. Most important of all he assured them that if they lived the AA program they would remain abstinent. Most patients remember the closing with which he often ended his lectures: "In recovery we are given floods of grace."

Because of his in-depth knowledge of alcoholism and his own personal recovery experience, West readily understood that chemical dependency was not just a physical problem needing medical attention but a mental and spiritual one as well. He had a profound knowledge of the meaning and the importance of the AA program and philosophy as the agent for the restoration of mental health, for the spiritual experience that brings about the personality change necessary for a *wholesome* recovery. In the Ford Center pamphlet *Alcoholism and the AA Program,* he writes eloquently of the power of the Twelve Steps:

> The whole "program" (of rehabilitation) operates in a social atmosphere of acceptance. This atmosphere of acceptance is, in itself, a beneficial factor in the treatment of the alcoholic, who is basically lonesome. At the beginning, it is necessary, according to the psychiatrist and good friend of AA, that two things take

place before recovery can occur in the alcoholic. These are, first, that the alcoholic must surrender, without reservation, the irrational desire to run things, to dominate people, and to influence events, and secondly, that one must undergo a deep inner change identified with a spiritual force. . . . This surrender takes place within the depths of the alcoholic's being, if one is to get well. . . . Dr. William James, a psychologist from Harvard University, writes in his book *A Variety of Religious Experiences* that this surrender and a spiritual experience are somewhat the same, in that they occur, many times, in the depths of despair. A true surrender probably occurs when the alcoholic recognizes that one's plight is hopeless. This insight is probably necessary for true recovery from alcoholism. We start by seeing that our lives are out of control. We can't avoid that first drink. We are powerless. This conviction must be deep. Its meaning must be clear. Our individual experiences have proven to us that we have no real defense against this disease. If these thoughts are what we know to be the truth about ourselves, we have surrendered.[4]

Ford Center Training Department

West's knowledge and expertise helped maintain cordial relations with the medical staff at the Eisenhower Medical Center. His outstanding surgical career earned him respect from the medical staff, which made it easier for them to accept his expertise in alcoholism, even though they did not know enough about the field themselves to be able to evaluate his skills. Having worked with the medical staff at the Little Company of Mary and at Cook County Hospital in Chicago, West was accustomed to the lack of knowledge, the hesitation, and even the indifference about alcoholism among the medical profession.

In 1986, West was instrumental in the startup of the Professionals in Residence Program, which offers professionals in the health care and social science fields the opportunity to spend ten days (later reduced to five) experiencing what it is like to be a patient at the Ford Center. The professionals also participate in staff activities to learn firsthand about the center's multidisciplinary approach to treatment. Lectures provide participants with the theoretical background upon which treatment is based.

Two years later, West started the Summer Institute for Medical Students. Out of 125 applicants the first year, 24 students were accepted from throughout the United States and Puerto Rico. The program is a hands-on learning model. It offers the medical students who go through the inpatient treatment units or the family program a thorough combination of formal education and participation in the patient experience. The students spend between ten and fourteen hours daily experiencing the treatment program. A majority of the day is spent following the patient schedule, but each student also attends structured learning sessions presented by the staff, who provide insight into addictive diseases and their treatment by a multidisciplinary team.

In 1987 West notified Betty Ford and John Schwarzlose that he intended to retire as medical director of the Betty Ford Center, effective January 1989. He continues to serve, however, as director of Outpatient Services and has served on the Board of Directors of the Betty Ford Center since 1988, of which he became vice-chairman

Former President Gerald Ford, Dr. James West, and Mrs. Betty Ford at the dedication of the James W. West Training Center, part of the Betty Ford Center in Rancho Mirage, California. Courtesy Betty Ford Center

in 1995. He also serves on the Board of Directors of the Eisenhower Memorial Hospital and of the Annenberg Center for Health Services, both of which are part of the Eisenhower Medical Center.

West's knowledge and wisdom about chemical dependency and its treatment have been gathered in a little volume published in 1997 called the *Book of Answers: Help for Those Struggling with Substance Abuse—and for the People Who Love Them.*

Betty Ford found in West a "healer, teacher, and friend" and endorsed naming one of the buildings on the campus the James W. West Training Center.

Notes

1. Ernest Kurtz, *Not-God: A History of Alcoholics Anonymous* (Center City, Minn.: Hazelden, 1979), 79–80.
2. James W. West, M.D., "Alcoholism—A General Hospital Meets the Challenge." *Illinois Medical Journal* 146, no. 2 (August 1974).
3. James W. West, M.D., "Social Setting Alcohol Detoxication: A Chicago Model." *Illinois Medical Journal* 150, no. 6 (December 1976).
4. *Alcoholism and the A.A. Program* (Rancho Mirage, Calif.: Betty Ford Center), 9–10.

Social Setting Alcohol Detoxication
A Chicago Model
BY JAMES W. WEST, M.D./CHICAGO

The treatment of acute alcoholism is a medical process which includes identifying the condition, assessing its urgency and making a disposition of the case. Acute alcoholism, defined as any degree of acute intoxication from alcohol, or one of the stages of the withdrawal syndrome, occurs at all levels of society. The vast majority of persons with this condition recover in their homes; rarely are they sufficiently sick to be admitted to a hospital. However, the treatment of acute alcoholism in those areas of the city where there occur concentrations of persons classified as the "homeless inebriate," presents unique problems hitherto handled in Illinois by the criminal justice system. Specifically, the police would pick up the public inebriate who was incapacitated in a public place, and after determining that he did not require hospitalization, would place him in the jail on a charge of public intoxication. Very few persons required hospital care so the jail, or "drunk tank" was the place where these homeless persons were housed. This system prevailed until the implementation of the Alcoholism and Intoxication Treatment Act (PA 78-1270)[1] in Illinois, on July 1, 1976. This act states, in effect, that alcoholism and intoxication are concerns of the health care system rather than the criminal justice system.

The new law demanded that the public inebriate be taken to a health care facility rather than the jail, and since few require hospital care, a new solution had to be designed. This solution took the form of the Social Setting Detoxication Center.

The concept of non-hospital, non-drug detoxication centers originated in Canada[2] and was further developed in California.[3] The purpose of the detoxication facility is detoxication and

Originally published in Illinois Medical Journal *150, no. 6 (December 1976).*
Reprinted with permission from the Illinois State Medical Society.

referral. It has a unique staffing pattern of trained persons, and exists in an alcoholism treatment network which includes the general hospital with which it has a close contractual relationship. It must be considered a medical facility inasmuch as its method of operation is clinical, and, with regard to alcoholism, it is an extension of the general hospital emergency room. The social setting detoxication facility and the back-up general hospital are intrinsic components of a network[4] which also includes rehabilitation centers, out-patient programs and vocational rehabilitation facilities.

The Chicago model of this concept of care is called Haymarket House, located at 12 South Peoria Street, serving the area of West Madison Street, a long time "skid row" section. The facility is operated by the Chicago Clergy Association for the Homeless Person, Inc. It was founded to function as a demonstration project by a private grant from the Chicago Community Trust, for the six month period before the implementation of the law PL 78-1270. Since July 1, 1976 the facility operates by a grant from the Illinois Department of Mental Health and Developmental Disabilities.

Haymarket House operates at two organizational levels, administrative and clinical. The administrative organization expedites the functions of the house and handles its relationships with the outside agencies, hospitals, and referral sites. The clinical staff of the house consists of triage and detoxication technicians and alcoholism counsellors. The clinical staff undergoes an initial training and this continues at a bimonthly period. The training and clinical competence levels are the responsibility of the Medical Consultant. The clinical personnel are recovered alcoholics, most of whom have had some experience in a "skid row" setting. The training follows a specific format, and consists of development of correct attitudes toward the client, and an understanding of the effective influence that the environment of a social setting detoxication facility has on the detoxifying person. The training also includes specific clinical diagnostic information[5] and demonstration to insure that the staff is proficient in triageing the client, that is: determining the nature of the disability, assessing its urgency and making a judgement as to disposition for care. Finally, all members of the house staff, including administration, must earn a certificate for having attended and demonstrated capability in cardio-pulmonary resuscitation. This latter training is provided by the American Heart Association.

Chart No. 1

Incoming Referrals (January–June, 1976)

	Jan.	Feb.	March	April	May	June
Police Dept.	193	290	470	433	400	355
Cook County Hospital	5	8	4	5	7	2
University of Ill. Hospital	3	3		9	1	4
Total	201	301	474	477	408	361

Chart No. 2

Discharges (January–June, 1976)

	Jan.	Feb.	March	April	May	June	Sub-Total	Percentage
Medical Emergency	7	7	14	12	10	7	57	2.6
Refused Referral	105	203	362	334	298	252	1554	70.8
Refused Referral Left Against Advice	6	2	7	10	12	23	60	2.7
Accepted Referral	73	76	82	79	58	69	437	20.0
Work	5	5	8	5	3	5	31	1.4
Home	5	6	6	16	19	3	55	2.5
Total	201	299	479	456	400	359	2194	100.0

Chart No. 6

Emergency Medical Admissions (January–June, 1976)

	Jan.	Feb.	March	April	May	June
Cook County Hospital	4	5	8	6	7	5
University of Illinois Hospital	3	2	6	6	3	2
Total	7	7	14	12	10	7
% of Total Residents	3.4	2.3	2.9	2.7	2.5	2.0

The actual process of care of the client begins at the police patrol wagon in which the police transport the client to Haymarket House (see Chart No. 1) after they have determined that his condition does not warrant taking him to a hospital. Incidentally, this triage function has been done successfully for many years by the policeman who still has to decide whether or not to bring the public inebriate directly to a hospital. At the entrance to Haymarket House the intake person, who is a triage and detoxication technician, assesses the client and determines his suitability for social setting detoxication. If there is any doubt as to an illness or injury which might threaten the health of the client, other than acute intoxication, the client is transported to the back-up hospital for a medical evaluation. Less than 5% (see Chart Nos. 2, 6) of the clients have required this hospital evaluation. At intake a brief history and other data are recorded and the client allowed to recline in a holding area, where the initial stages of detoxication occur. As soon as a client is able to function well enough he is showered, deloused and given clean clothes. He is then moved to another area where he can socialize with other clients and where counselling and group therapy take place. During the period of recovery from acute intoxication the staff member makes frequent checks on the client for any aberration of vital signs which may signal a health or life threatening complication. The philosophy of the clinical staff is that if one is in doubt about a client's physical condition, he is to be transported immediately to the back-up hospital for an examination. Those conditions which have accounted for the decision to transport the client for medical care are seizure activity, injuries discovered after admission to the facility, precordial pain, respiratory difficulty, or a history of some severe medical condition such as diabetes or heart disease.[6] The staff also includes a blood pressure test, temperature and a testape urinalysis in the general assessment of the client. Those clients who stay for more than 24 hours are transported to the local Health Department Clinic for a chest X-ray.

Chart No. 3

Length of Stay (January–June, 1976)

	Jan.	Feb.	March	April	May	June	Sub-Total	Percentage
Over 5 days	38	12	29	27	19	23	148	6.8
3–5 days	34	28	24	39	40	23	188	8.6
2–4 days	8	20	25	26	24	17	120	5.5
1–2 days	25	19	14	22	11	15	106	4.9
Sub-Total (Over 1 day)	105	79	92	114	94	78	562	25.8
12–24 hours	38	85	162	86	103	70	544	25.0
5–12 hours	26	80	111	141	137	177	672	31.0
1–5 hours	32	47	105	115	66	34	399	18.3
Sub-Total (Under 1 day)	96	212	378	342	306	281	1615	74.2
Total	201	291	470	456	400	359	2177	100.00

Chart No. 4

Number of Times Admitted (January–June, 1976)

	Jan.	Feb.	March	April	May	June
1	156	176	187	162	134	140
2	31	64	90	69	63	56
3	10	29	58	52	38	24
4	3	16	43	43	26	28
5	1	9	28	31	22	12
6		4	23	23	26	6
7		2	15	14	22	13
8		1	12	14	13	10
9			7	7	9	14
10			5	7	5	8
11			3	7	5	7
12			2	5	5	7
13			1	4	4	8
14				3	8	6
15				2	6	5
16				2	4	4
17				2	5	2
18					2	3
19					1	4
20					1	2
20+						2

Chart No. 5

Outgoing Referrals (January–June, 1976)

	Jan.	Feb.	March	April	May	June
Salvation Army	9	9	16	11	6	8
Cathedral Shelter	11	2	2	1	3	
Christian Ind. Lg.	11	6	3	7	4	9
Holy Cross Mission	16	7	7	25	11	12
C.A.T.C.	7	5	6	7	6	6
Downey VA, ARP	12	10	11	8	7	11
Hines VA, ARP	1	10	15	3	4	7
Read Zone Center	1	5	3	4	7	
1919 W. Taylor	2	4	6	3		2
Manteno State Hospital Program		7		1	1	1
Elgin State Hospital Program		3	4	1		

After the acute intoxication or withdrawal state is managed, the client is encouraged to stay at the facility for counselling and referral. Statistically, the majority leave before 12 hours (see Chart No. 3), but of those who stay for a longer period, the referral rate approximates 70%. The number of times clients have been admitted ranges from once to more than twenty times (see Chart No. 4). A referral consists in transporting the client to a recognized rehabilitation center where arrangements have been made for his admission (see Chart No. 5). While awaiting referral, regular A.A. meetings, group therapy sessions, psychodrama, and individual counselling take place.

The six month experience as a demonstration project of Haymarket House has proved a number of things. First, the principle of a social setting detoxication treatment for acute alcoholism is a sound one.[6] Second, the use of drugs is not necessary at this level of acute alcoholism. Third, this class of clients with acute alcoholism shows a different clinical picture than the acute alcoholism sufferer in the private setting. This difference appears to take the form of a greater degree of incapacity on much less alcohol, and in consequence of this lower tolerance and less alcohol intake, a much shorter detoxication time with fewer and less intense symptoms of the acute withdrawal syndrome. A research project dealing with this particular phenomenon is being designed for study at Haymarket House. Fourth, the effectiveness of a social setting detoxication center for this population (see Chart No's. 7, 8, 9) must be judged on its ability to detoxify clients, and not on its ability to rehabilitate, which is an altogether different function not suited to the purpose of a detoxication facility. Fifth and finally, the Social Setting Detoxication Center, as an effective part of the alcoholism treatment network, acts as an entry point into long term care for an appreciable percentage of previously "hopeless" and homeless persons.

Chart No. 7

Race and Nationality (January–June, 1976)

	Jan.	Feb.	March	April	May	June	Sub-Total	Percentage
Negro	40	63	71	93	98	91	456	20.8
Caucasian	128	189	339	299	246	223	1424	65.0
Spanish Surname	19	19	21	11	20	17	107	4.9
American Indian	14	30	43	44	44	30	205	9.3
Total	201	301	474	447	408	361	2192	100.0

Ages by Decades	20's	30's	40's	50's	60's	70's	80's
	5%	17.3%	32.6%	31%	11%	2.6%	.01%

Youngest	20 years old
Oldest	82 years old

Chart No. 8

Marital Status (January–June, 1976)
Based On New Admissions Only

	Jan.	Feb.	March	April	May	June	Sub-Total	Percentage
Married	11	8	12	15	10	14	70	7.3
Single	83	90	98	89	49	73	482	50.5
Divorced	51	56	58	33	43	40	281	29.4
Separated	7	13	6	11	15	7	59	6.2
Widower	4	9	13	14	17	6	63	6.6
Total	156	176	187	162	134	140	955	100.0

Chart No. 9

Veteran Status (Based On New Admissions Only) (January–June, 1976)

	Jan.	Feb.	March	April	May	June
Veterans	81	103	124	105	91	96
Non-Veterans	30	51	43	51	43	44
No Information	45	22	20	6		
Total	156	176	187	162	134	140

References

1. Alcoholism and Intoxication Treatment Act PA 78-1270. As amended by PA 79-59.
2. Addiction Research Institute, *Detoxication Programs,* Toronto, Canada.
3. Robert G. O'Briant, M.D. "Social Setting Detoxication," *Alcohol and Research World;* Winter 1974/1975.
4. James W. West, M.D., "The General Hospital—Its Place in the Alcoholism Treatment Network." To be published in the *Journal of Alcohol Studies.* Submitted 1976.
5. Knott, David H., M.D., Ph.D.; James D. Beard, Ph.D.; Robert D. Fink, M.D.; "Acute Withdrawal From Alcohol." *Emergency Medicine,* February, 1974.
6. M. J. Ashley et al. "Skid Row Alcoholism," *Archives of Internal Medicine* 136: 272–278, March 1976.
7. Robert O'Briant, M.D.; N. William Petersen, "Medical Evaluation of the Safety of Non-Hospital Detoxication," 1335 Guerrero St., San Francisco, California.

Alcoholism—A General Hospital Meets the Challenge
BY JAMES W. WEST, M.D./EVERGREEN PARK

The program at Little Company of Mary Hospital, Evergreen Park, for the care of alcoholism patients can serve as a model for any general hospital. The prevalence of alcoholism accounts for about 30% of all general hospital admissions. Although the primary diagnosis for these patients may not be specified as "alcoholism," the reason for hospitalization is usually related to alcohol use.

There are three important factors which have emerged in our society to hasten our directly addressing the responsibility for the care of the alcoholism patient. These factors include, firstly, "Legal Power" which has resulted in the Uniform Practice Act removing the inebriate from the criminal justice system making him a responsibility of the health care system. In addition, there have been successful malpractice litigations for refusal to treat the alcoholic patient.

Secondly, there is "Green Power," money, provided by health insurance carriers, who, by law, must cover the treatment of alcoholism as new insurance contracts are written. In addition, Federal legislation provides $375 million in the next two years for both alcoholism care and the training of health care professionals.

Thirdly, there is "People Power," a new attitude by the public about this sickness. Educational information has helped people recognize alcoholism as an illness for which they expect the best possible treatment as they do with any other sickness.

At Little Company of Mary Hospital, a plan was put into operation which provides care for the acutely ill alcoholism patient and initiates his long term recovery through a system of inpatient services and effective after-care referral relationships. This program functions with the support and participation of

Originally published in Illinois Medical Journal *146, no. 2 (August 1974). Reprinted with permission from the Illinois State Medical Society.*

Administration, Medical Staff, Nursing Services and the Department of Patient and Family Counseling.

The start of the program at Little Company of Mary Hospital was preceeded by a period of inservice training, participated in by emergency care personnel and members of the Nursing Services Department. The training program included lectures and discussions about the nature of the disease and a review of its spectrum of treatment. Attitudes of the treatment personnel were particularly stressed. Bedside teaching of nurses, residents and interns and frequent review of each patient's responses to treatment is an intrinsic part of the program.

Patients are admitted to the hospital with the diagnosis of "alcoholism—acute withdrawal syndrome." The patients are placed on the medical service and their treatment is reviewed, as with other illnesses, by the Department of Internal Medicine.

The treatment program in this hospital is an organized multidisciplinary diagnostic and therapeutic system. The admitting physician retains the primary responsibility for the care of the alcoholism patient, but shares the treatment effort with a team of professionals who participate in the various aspects of the recovery procedure process. The sophisticated medical back-up systems are entirely adequate to properly serve the acutely ill alcoholism patient in the community. A long-term alcoholism rehabilitation unit, or an isolated unit for the care of the short-term alcoholic, is not necessary. The hospital can meet its community needs without the addition of any medical beds by treating acute alcoholism patients in the regular medical beds without isolating them from other medical patients. Adequate medical management makes this system of patient distribution practical. Empathetic and informed nursing care along with adequate medication have proven this system to be feasible by a large experience.

The actual system of care begins with the emergency room procedures. Transportation of the patient is usually by police vehicle or private auto. Upon arrival, immediate care of the patient is begun with the triage process wherein the diagnosis is made, the urgency of the patient's condition is determined and the type of care is assigned.

At Little Company of Mary Hospital, urgency of care is determined by assessing which stage of acute withdrawal from alcohol exists. A person who is merely intoxicated, but not suffering from withdrawal systems, is usually not in need of hospital admission unless there is some additional pathologic process which might be aggravated seriously by the alcohol.

The phases of withdrawal from alcohol are the conditions which are potentially health or even life threatening. These conditions invariably follow prolonged ingestion of large amounts of alcohol. The emergency department uses the following staging system in processing the acute alcoholism patient:

Stage I consists of psychomotor agitation (the "shakes"), autonomic hyperactivity (tachycardia, hypertension, hyperhidrosis and anorexia).

Stage II consists of hallucinations—these are auditory, visual or tactile; there may be one or a combination of these. The hallucinatory experience is usually frightening and there is usually an amnesia for details of this experience. However, the patient is oriented as to time, place and person.

Stage III consists of delusions, disorientation, delirium, plus all of the above, with severe psychomotor agitation. This may be intermitent, but is always followed by amnesia.

Stage IV consists of convulsive seizure activity.

The management of the patient is determined by the stage of the acute withdrawal syndrome that exists. Usually, the Stage I withdrawal patient may be discharged with a mild medication and be followed in an out-patient treatment setting. The usual medication used for this situation is hydroxyzine (Vistaril®), in modest amounts, and a one day supply to be renewed by the physician at the outpatient clinic when the patient returns the next day. This stage may be unpredictably progressive so, if a patient gives a history of having previously experienced seizures during withdrawal, he is admitted for a 24 to 48 hour period. Seizures show a 70% recurrence rate with each withdrawal experience.

Since hallucinatory activity of Stage II frequently proceeds to the next and much more serious Stage III, these Stage II patients are admitted to the hospital. Both Stage II and Stage III are treated with adequate sedation to control the psychomotor agitation and a neuroleptic agent (chlorpromazine [Thorazine®], or haloperiodol [Haldol®]) to manage the hallucinatory phenomena. The Stage III patient is usually very ill. This state has been traditionally described as the D.T.'s. Stage III is rarely due to alcohol alone; trauma, infection, multiple drug use, hypovolemia or electrolyte imbalance are usually also present.

Stage IV acute withdrawal states are characterized by seizures which are controlled by diazepam (Valium®), or some other anticonvulsant agent. Sodium diphenylhydantoin (Dilantin Sodium) is not effective for about 72 hours.

This method of emergency room staging has made the processing of the acutely ill alcoholic a more effective procedure. All of the physicians and the nurses in the Emergency Department are familiar with the diagnostic criteria of this system. Appropriate treatment starts in the Emergency Room consistent with the exact nature and urgency of the condition.

Those Stage II, III, and IV patients, all of whom are admitted to the hospital, are given medication while still in the emergency room. When the patient exhibits an intense psychomotor state, he is usually held in the emergency area until he responds to the medication.

All persons who are admitted do so voluntarily. When there is an acute bed shortage, Stage I and Stage II patients are referred to other hospitals where arrangements have been made to accept these referrals.

Admission procedures include using the diagnosis of "acute alcoholism—withdrawal syndrome." The patients are admitted to the medical areas where they are placed with the other medical patients. The additional use of medication has effectively eliminated the use of physical restraints, except in the rare and short term use of a waist Posey belt in the Stage III patient. A set of standing orders, which have been the focus of inservice training, gives the nursing personnel the use of sedation as they see the need for the patient. Although there are many effective drugs for use in the withdrawal syndrome, one drug has been chosen so that all those who administer it can become familiar with its effectiveness and its limitations. This drug chlordiazepoxide (Librium®) has had wide use and its limitations and safety features are well known. After the patient has recovered from the acute withdrawal syndrome, he is taken off all sedation. Occasionally he may continue the use of a neuroleptic or an anticonvulsant drug if this is indicated. If a patient suffers from concommitant physical disorders, they are treated simultaneously with the withdrawal therapy.

Three considerations in the treatment of the acute withdrawal syndrome should be mentioned. These are, effects of withdrawal on 1) central nervous system, 2) fluid and electrolyte balance, and 3) abnormal glucose metabolism.

The central nervous system demands immediate attention in the form of adequate sedation to combat the psychomotor activity. This condition is probably due in part to an increase in intracellular sodium and a decrease in intracellular potassium brought about by alcohol and its effect on mitochondria produced ATPase. This enzyme, a necessary part of the active transport system within the cell membrane, keeps the sodium and potassium ratio in a correct state. An abnormal ratio reduces transcellular membrane potentials thus increasing excitability of nerve and muscle tissue. Sedation controls this condition of tissue excitability, and abstinence from alcohol usually restores transcellular electrical gradients within a day or two of treatment. Dilantin Sodium is given to those patients who have seizures or who have a history of seizures. This is given with phenobarbital for the first 72 hours, after which Dilantin Sodium can be given alone. Dilantin Sodium affects cell membrane physiology by decreasing intracellular sodium and increasing intracellular potassium, thus effectively counteracting one of the most prominent causes of psychomotor hyperactivity in alcohol withdrawal.

Fluid balance, contrary to traditional beliefs, is in a state of overhydration. Only when the blood alcohol level is rising is the antidiuretic hormone of the posterior pituitary suppressed producing a diuresis, mostly a free water clearance with some magnesium loss. The other electrolytes, sodium, potassium and chloride, are retained. There is retention of water and electrolytes after the blood alcohol level reaches a plateau, which is usually early in a drinking episode. Thus, when the patient is admitted to the hospital, he is in positive water balance and, because he has also retained his electrolytes, he is in a state of iso-osmotic overhydration. Unless the patient has been vomiting, or has had a diarrhea, intravenous fluids are contraindicated. The patient can usually tolerate orally whatever fluids he needs. Diuresis occurs shortly after withdrawal from alcohol has started, which restores fluid and electrolyte balance to normal levels. Magnesium levels may be low, but replacement by I.M. solution has not been done on this program since its value is controversial.

Abnormal carbohydrate metabolism is associated with labile blood glucose levels. Alcohol depletes hepatic glycogen stores, impairs gluconeogenesis, and produces an occasional hypoglycemia of such a low level as to produce seizure activity. Blood sugar levels are followed carefully for the first four days.

Other conditions which demand careful watching are infections, possible trauma, or other physical conditions which, in common with the acute withdrawal state, can precipitate a sudden Stage III condition with delusion, delirium, hallucination and other signs recognized traditionally as the D.T.'s. There are some warning signals for this stage of withdrawal which the alert physician or nurse can recognize and treat promptly.

Standing orders, which are meant to serve as a grade and base line procedure, have been reviewed with all the personnel who will deal with the patient. These standing orders have served a large number of patients and they are designed to be modified to meet the individual needs of each patient.

The following is the order sheet for patients admitted for acute alcoholism:

ADMITTING DIAGNOSIS:

Acute Alcoholism
Acute Withdrawal Syndrome—Alcohol
Other Medical or traumatic conditions if present

ADMISSION ORDERS:	LABORATORIES:
STAT	DRAW IN A.M., FOLLOWING DAY
CBC	SMA 12/60
Urinalysis	S.I.C.D.
Blood Drug Screen	S.G.P.T.
Glucose	Triglycerides
Blood Alcohol	Coagulation Survey
Chest X-ray	ECG
Electrolytes	Bland or General Diet as tolerated

MEDICATIONS AND NURSING:

Start in Emergency Department

1. Inj. Librium® 50 mg. IM. STAT: and 50 mg. of Librium® may be repeated every one/half hour if patient is very restless.
2. Inj. Librium® 50 mg. IM. every 3 to 4 hours; but do not awaken patient if asleep. (This dosage to be changed as indicated)
3. Inj. Sodium Amytal® gr. iii IM. at about 10:00 p.m. for sleep if necessary.
4. Inj. Thaimine Hydrochloride® 200 mg. IM. b.i.d.
5. Take Berminal "500"® b.i.d.

6. Have relative remain with the patient after patient reaches the floor until nurse indicates this is no longer needed.
7. Do not use restraints.
8. Notify physician about admission and patient's condition and call physician's resident or intern.
9. Observe patient closely for any rise in temperature, or profuse perspiration, or hallucinations, as these signs may indicate impending Stage III Withdrawal. Notify physician or his resident.
10. Daily therapy sessions at 1:45 p.m. in North Pavilion, Room 226, Patient and Family Counseling Department.
11. AA Meetings on MONDAY, WEDNESDAY, FRIDAY EVENINGS. 8:00 p.m. (MONDAY AND FRIDAY in Meeting Room "B"—Wednesday in Board Room)
12. Further workup as indicated.
13. Notify Alcoholism Program Coordinator of patient's admission.

Psychosocial therapy begins on admissions of the patient to the emergency care system. This starts with the same caring and accepting attitude as the nurse or physician would have with any other kind of illness. The patient is assured of help and relief by personnel who understand that their approach is effective in allaying fears and damping psychomotor agitation. 95% of alcoholism patients enter psychosocial treatment by way of some physical or acute social crisis. Their initial contact with the helping professional may set the direction of their eventual recovery process.

At Little Company of Mary Hospital the psychosocial therapy begins on admission and continues throughout the patient's stay. The physician counsels daily with the patient, outlining the physical effects of alcohol use and helping to plan goals for rehabilitation. An alcoholism program coordinator sees each patient soon after admission and daily thereafter, explaining the alcoholism program, providing literature and discussing the AA and Alanon programs. The patient's family is involved in the program by introduction to Alanon groups.

Group Therapy

Group therapy has been found to be the most effective alcoholism treatment modality and the patient is introduced to this as soon as he is physically able to attend. Some patients are brought by wheel chair to the daily sessions. This therapy consists of didactic sessions given by a physician covering the physical effects of alcohol use. Group psychotherapy, conducted by trained alcoholism therapists, uses the orthodox psychotherapeutic techniques including transactional analysis, group process, communication and some psychodrama. AA meetings take place on three evenings a week at the hospital and are participated in by the patients and community members of AA. Film presentations on alcoholism for staff and patients are shown and discussed. These films are produced by the American Hospital Association and are provided by the South Suburban Council on Alcoholism as a service to the community. A workshop group takes place on Saturday for patients and ex-patients. The goal of this session is insight development, particularly as it pertains to alcoholism in the patient's life and family. Alanon groups for spouses of patients meet on the hospital campus once a week.

Psychometric testing is done on those patients designated as needing this by the physician. These include the Bender-Gestalt, the Shipley-Raven Matrix and the M.M.P.I. tests. Psychiatric consultation is available and used on very depressed and otherwise psychiatrically disturbed patients. Some psychiatrists have referred their alcoholism patients to the alcoholism program in the medical section. They thus conserve the psychiatric beds for their patients who require confined care.

After-care is an essential component of any acceptable alcoholism program. This consists of directing and following, or referring, the patient for continuing alcoholism therapy, the intensity of which is dependent on the individual need.

At Little Company of Mary Hospital, the acute care program is necessarily of short duration. As soon as the patient is no longer in need of physical treatment, he is directed into the after-care system. While in the hospital, he is introduced to the psychosocial system of therapy in which he will hopefully participate for the rest of his life. This kind of treatment addresses itself to the disease, alcoholism.

The process of after-care begins with the patient calling the local AA office on the day before discharge. This assures that members of AA in the patient's community will contact the patient and bring him to the local AA group meetings after he is discharged from the hospital. Arrangements are also made for outpatient counseling with the professional people who run the hospital group therapy sessions. The Department of Patient and Family Counseling provides family and patient counseling to those who need this service. During the hospital stay, the social worker for the alcoholism program works with the patient to solve those problems that the individual may present as part of his total alcoholic career. Some of these patients brought in by police are in need of post-hospital living accommodations or nursing home care.

There are some patients who are in need of longer inpatient care in the form of rehabilitation. These patients are transferred to one of the excellent rehabilitation centers in the city for a continuation of the psychosocial therapy to which the patient was introduced at Little Company of Mary Hospital.

Goals and expectations of this program consist of a recovery rate which is acceptable for an effective alcoholism program. This general hospital program is not a short time treatment process, but must be looked upon as the entry point to long term treatment, either as an outpatient with AA involvement and professional counseling, or as an inpatient in one of the alcoholism rehabilitation centers.

Summary

This care of alcoholism will conform to the standards of such care set by the Joint Commission on Accreditation of Hospitals. The two components of care which this, and any other general hospital can provide, are emergency care and after-care.

Some of more elaborate psychosocial group therapeutics at Little Company of Mary Hospital would not be necessary for all general hospital programs. Local volunteer AA people from the community can provide much good counseling and many hospitals now have AA groups which meet in the hospital area. Ideally, every general hospital should take care of the acute alcoholism patient in the community, and establish an after-care system which would include an alcoholism rehabilitation center to which patients, who require more than a short inpatient experience, could be referred. A good rehabilitation center can serve a constellation of referring general hospitals. General hospitals would then be providers of acute care for which most of them have been designed.

This program for the general hospital care of acute alcoholism has served a large number of patients and is proving to be a feasible method of serving its community. The average daily census of acute alcoholism patients in this 550 bed hospital runs about 6 patients. This census figure remains generally low because of the short stay. The therapy sessions are also attended by those patients who are in the hospital for other conditions, but who suffer concomitantly from alcoholism, or whose alcoholism has been uncovered by a perceptive physician.

Finally, training opportunities are available for physicians and other professionals, so that all general hospitals, who seek to meet the challenge of treating their community alcoholism patients, can attain this goal.

References

Block, Marvin A., M.D., *Alcoholism—Its Facets and Phases,* John Day Co.

Guyton, Arthur C., M.D., *Medical Physiology,* W. B. Saunders Co.,
    1971.
Knott, David H., M.D., Ph.D., James D. Beard, Ph.D., Robert D.
    Fink, M.D., "Acute Withdrawal from Alcohol," *Emergency
    Medicine,* February, 1974.
Knott, David H., M.D., Ph.D., James D. Beard, Ph.D., "The
    Diagnosis and Therapy of Acute Withdrawal from Alcohol,"
    Current Psychiatric Therapies, Vol. 10, 1970.
Lesesne, Henry R., M.D., Harold J. Fallon, M.D., "Alcoholic Liver
    Disease," *Post Graduate Medicine,* January, 1973.
Myerson, Ralph M., M.D., "Metabolic Aspects of Alcohol and Their
    Biological Significance," *Medical Clinics of North America,*
    Vol. 57, No. 4.
West, James W., M.D., "New Program for Alcoholics—The
    Treatment of Alcoholism in a General Hospital," *Pacemaker,*
    Little Company of Mary Hospital, Vol. VI, No. 1, 1974.
Yalom, Irving D., *The Theory and Practice of Group Psychotherapy,*
    Basic Books, Inc., Library of Congress, Catalog No. 7194305,
    1970.

Alcoholism and the A.A. Program
BY A DOCTOR IN A.A.

Drinking for enjoyment is socially and personally acceptable for twelve out of thirteen persons in the United States. The thirteenth person no longer enjoys drinking, nor is the drinking socially acceptable. His drinking is destructive to himself, and harmful to others. Though he may know this, he cannot stop drinking. He is an alcoholic.

I am one of these thirteenth persons. I have lots of company; in fact this "thing" that I have, called alcoholism, is the fourth most common disease in the United States. The word, disease, is particularly interesting to me, because I am a physician and my business is the recognition and treatment of illnesses. Before joining A.A. some years ago, I knew little about alcoholism, although I was its victim. Today, I recognize it as a specific disease, as does the American Medical Association and other organizations who concern themselves with illnesses. I, somehow, knew that I was not sick because I drank, but that I drank because I was sick. This concept led me to look further into the disease, that I might more surely cooperate with the Steps of recovery; to develop, as our friends the psychiatrists say: insight.

Alcoholism
Alcoholism is a disease, the most apparent symptom of which is intoxication. Coupled with this is a physical over-sensitivity to alcohol not found in non-alcoholic persons. An alcoholic is defined as a person whose drinking interferes frequently or constantly with one's important life adjustments and functions.

The cause of this disease is unknown. As with other diseases, such as epilepsy, schizophrenia, cancer, etcetera, the exact cause has never been determined. We do know, however, that it affects every strata of society. It is no respecter of persons or status. As

Originally published by the Betty Ford Center (Rancho Mirage, Calif.) Reprinted with permission from the Betty Ford Center.

a matter of fact, even knowing a great deal about the illness does not confer immunity. Some of my close friends in A.A. are psychiatrists whose knowledge of alcoholism was profound, although this did not arrest their illness. It is certain, however, that there are components within the personality that "set the person up" for alcoholism. This mental peculiarity has been called "the soil for addiction." Probably in the make-up of the alcoholic, in the tenseness and inner unrest, there exists a condition which is relieved by drink, and which, once relieved, establishes the addiction. It would be interesting to try to find out what we look for in the drink. A prominent psychologist, after questioning many alcoholics, has been able to summarize this particular desire: "I want to be myself, free and easy to seek the things I want; harmony within, and to be at peace with the world."

Paradoxically, drinking takes away our freedom (we lose our choice as to whether we drink). We find more mental pain in the state to which we fled than the uncomfortable world we tried to escape. We learn, to our horror, that we cannot return to that world. We are captured, imprisoned, by alcoholism. We forget in our misery, though, that the world from which we fled was uncomfortable and distressing in the first place. It is this state of mind that exists before abnormal drinking starts, that we must try to change, lest we lose our sobriety and relapse into sick drinking for the same reason we started sick drinking in the first place.

The Personality of the Alcoholic

To gain insight, it would seem wise to consider carefully this commonly accepted list of personality traits found in the alcoholic. This person has certain characteristics or symptoms that occur in normal people, but in this case are exaggerated and uncontrolled. These are the things that render one incapable of being at peace. They compel one to seek relief. They lie beneath the surface of the exterior, and, when in operation, drive one to drink in spite of all that the individual may know that drinking will produce in the way of self-destruction and harm.

Low frustration tolerance seems to be about the most constant trait. This is the inability to endure for a length of time any uncomfortable circumstance or feeling. The alcoholic is impatient.

Anxiety, that state which seems to exist in all people, exists in an exaggerated way in the alcoholic. This person is subject to nameless dreads and fears. This anxiety drives the alcoholic to "fight or flight." Sometimes this is called free-floating anxiety. Usually the alcoholic is not even certain about that for which he or she should be anxious.

Grandiosity. This can be described as "the organization of the universe around the perpendicular pronoun." Grandiosity is worn as a protective armour to hide feelings of low self-esteem. In reality, although the alcoholic nourishes an inflated self-image, the deep conviction is one of self-worthlessness. The alcoholic quivers inside a bold and shiny suit of armour. The person feels inadequate, but can't dare show it.

Perfectionism sets impossible goals with inevitable failures and resultant guilt. The alcoholic is an idealist. This idealism, perhaps, is one of the reasons for success after recovery has been initiated. The alcoholic is an exceptionally fine worker once the illness has been arrested and after perfectionism has been reduced to reasonable proportions.

Wishful thinking. We alcoholics are masters at this. Wishful thinking is the science of arranging to do what we want to do, then making it appear reasonable. This keeps our technique of rationalization operating smoothly. Half truths, or none at all, permeate this trait.

Isolation and deep insecurity deprive us of the real generosity needed to make close and enduring friendships. We are loners.

Sensitivity. This exaggerates all the unpleasant interpersonal relationships we experience. We have all been through the occasional snub, not necessarily meant by the other person, and have dwelt upon this event until it becomes a downright resentment.

Impulsiveness. "I want what I want when I want it." This is probably related in some way to a low frustration tolerance that we all seem to have. In some ways the alcoholic takes a certain pride in this impulsiveness as though it were a valuable asset. The alcoholic can't seem to enjoy a job or task, and is preoccupied only with completing it. Much of what one does is done with an intensity that leaves the alcoholic emotionally exhausted. Long, tedious tasks are not for the alcoholic; rather there is a burst of effort which lasts until the fun is gone, or interest wanes.

Defiance is a characteristic, probably the result of unbearable conflict and anxiety, that makes itself evident when the alcoholic rejects society as a whole, both when drinking and not drinking. This is associated with a feeling that the person does not fit, exactly, into society.

Dependence on other persons exists in some form in all alcoholics.

These personality traits, then, all contribute to the mental make-up of the alcoholic. These same mental traits also contribute to make the alcoholic drink. Since these are the things about the alcoholic that make it such that one is unable to resist, or refrain from, the first drink, it stands to reason that sobriety must depend upon doing something about these characteristics. Before we consider recovery, however, let us consider the physical aspects of this disease.

Physical Aspects of Alcoholism

Alcoholism, though essentially a mental illness, has certain physical aspects. There is no known difference between the alcoholic and the non-alcoholic physically. It is only when the complications of prolonged alcoholic ingestion occur that physical signs appear. These findings, however, are not in themselves physical symptoms of the alcoholic, but the organic body changes that occur as a consequence of prolonged alcohol intake. This means that if the alcoholic stops drinking before these rather late complications occur, the person will have a perfectly normal physical make-up, entirely indistinguishable from the non-alcoholic person.

Whereas alcoholism is the fourth most common disease in the United States, its death rate rises to the third place. Death occurs from acute over-ingestion of alcohol, cirrhosis of the liver, suicide, traffic and highway accidents incurred while drunk, and acute withdrawal states accompanied by delirium tremens. In some instances, chronic disabilities, such as organic brain changes, result from drinking, and render the alcoholic a permanent mental invalid.

Following the start of recovery, it is only good sense to apply the simple rules of good physical hygiene, emphasizing adequate rest, exercise and diet. Although the alcoholic may have developed cirrhosis of the liver, life, with adequate medical attention, should be unhandicapped by this complication in most cases. Certainly, a real respect for sound physical health should be the attitude of all recovering alcoholics. Anyone's mental outlook is surely influenced by the feeling of physical well-being. The alcoholic should keep in mind that fatigue, especially when accompanied by some ego-deflating experience, can produce, and usually does, a state of irritability and depression.

As a member of A.A. gets older, regular physical check-ups are in order. The alcoholic whose illness has been arrested, should keep in mind that sound physical health contributes to the enjoyment of recovery.

Recovery from Alcoholism

The term "recovery" does not apply to alcoholism as it does to other diseases. Recovery usually means that the disease is eradicated, the patient is cured. When we use the term "recovery" from alcoholism, we mean that the symptoms are arrested on a day-to-day basis. Alcoholism is incurable, but drinking can be permanently arrested and the disturbing personality traits which cause it, greatly alleviated.

Recovery from alcoholism has no doubt occurred throughout the centuries. There are four forms that recovery takes. There is that exceptional and rare case where spontaneous and instant change in a personality has occurred, associated with some spiritual experience. There are also those people who finally decide to "go on the wagon." This abstinence from alcohol may be supplemented by a drug designed to make the person sick if one takes a drink. Since this particular form of recovery consists of eliminating only one symptom of alcoholism, the sobriety is not only uncomfortable, but negative and almost always temporary. There is also that approach to recovery wherein the patient cooperates with psychiatric treatment, and in so doing develops insights into the illness and follows suggestions as to recovery. The rate of recovery from this method is necessarily low due to the inability of the busy psychiatrist to devote enough time to the individual alcoholic. Furthermore, the alcoholic is frequently less than completely honest with his physician-psychiatrist. The most successful approach to the treatment of alcoholism has been A.A. This has been the agent for the restoration of mental health, sufficient to permanently arrest drinking, in more than half of those alcoholics who expose themselves to it.

Before any therapy will help, the alcoholic must stop drinking. The most valuable asset at the beginning of recovery must be a strong desire to stop drinking and to stay stopped. Recovery through A.A. includes a complete commitment to a program of twelve Steps. These Steps have a spiritual basis, they use psychotherapeutic tools, and they operate in an environment where the alcoholic feels a strong sense of acceptance. A.A., with its spiritual basis, implies that God plays a major role in the recovery of the patient. Communication with God is established in the first few Steps. The next few Steps use a natural means to bring about the changes necessary in the personality of the alcoholic, the psychotherapeutic tools we spoke of above. The whole "program" operates in a social atmosphere of acceptance. This atmosphere of acceptance is, in itself, a beneficial factor in the treatment of the alcoholic, who is basically lonesome. At the beginning, it is necessary, according to a psychiatrist and good friend of A.A., that two things take place before recovery can occur in the alcoholic. These are, first, that the alcoholic must surrender, without reservation, the irrational desire to run things, to dominate people, and to influence events, and secondly, that one must undergo a deep inner change identified with a spiritual force. A very necessary part of recovery, then, includes surrender. This surrender takes place within the depth of the alcoholic's being, if one is to get well. It is different than submission, for though the alcoholic may wish to get better, if response to this wish is merely submission, the person is not ready for recovery. As a matter of fact, according to some authorities, surrender, when it occurs, takes place within the subconscious. It is not a thing that can be desired and gained merely by wishing. It occurs as a thing over which the victim has little control. Dr. William James, a psychologist from Harvard University, writes in his book "A Variety of Religious Experiences" that this surrender and a spiritual experience are somewhat the same, in that they occur, many times, in the depths of despair. A true surrender probably occurs when the alcoholic recognizes that one's plight is hopeless. This insight is probably necessary for true recovery from alcoholism. We start by seeing that our lives are out of control. We can't avoid that first drink. We are powerless. This conviction must be deep. Its meaning must be clear. Our individual experiences have proven to us that we have no real defense against this disease. If these thoughts are what we know to be the truth about ourselves, we have surrendered.

When we say that we came to believe that a Power greater than ourselves could restore us to sanity, we imply that we ourselves could not restore ourselves to sanity. We also mean that our insanity was not drunkenness, although this behavior was many times insane, but that our insanity included that period of time when we weren't intoxicated. It was the insanity, or the abnormal mental state that existed within ourselves, that made us take that first drink. It is this abnormal mental state, call it insanity, that we came to believe that God could remove.

The first act in A.A. is one wherein we, to the best of our ability, try to make our lives conform with what we think God would want us to do and be. Sometimes this is difficult to know, but we alcoholics realize that if we are willing to take this particular Step, it is apparently enough. Enlightenment as to His will for us gradually increases as our minds become more clear. In many alcoholics, this Step is accompanied by a sense of relief as they "let go." It is no longer necessary that they be "general managers of the universe." They are now under the new direction of Someone Who is All Powerful and communicates with them at the level of the conscience.

Having established a relationship which includes a dependence upon God, we next take measures which are recognized by the medical profession as effective therapeutic tools for restoring mental health. We must drop that protective armour, come out of our shells, exercise courage, and, with pencil in hand, record our defects. We prayerfully try to see where intolerance, wishful thinking, grandiosity, anxiety, impulsiveness, isolationism, and defiance, boil to the surface of our daily lives as dishonesty, fear, egocentricity and resentment. Had God wished to cure us with a wave of the hand, this inventory would not be necessary, but he has required that we cooperate in our recovery by using natural psychological means. This inventory takes time, a small price to pay for the arrest of this incurable illness. To be effective, some real soul-searching, done and recorded over a period of weeks or more, seems necessary. Recovery in depth is the goal. Sobriety of a temporary type (even years) may exist in the alcoholic who does not take this Step. Sobriety is precarious, when the alcoholic is repressing the symptoms and is wearing the mask of sanity. Recovery is superficial.

Alcoholism is not drunkenness, intoxication is only one symptom of alcoholism. One prominent psychiatrist states that he can tell the member who really "has" the program from the one who is only sober. The member who has recovered in depth is relaxed, and has an inner peace. This comes from a change in mental make-up through the application of these Steps which honestly face, record, and expose these defects which constitute the alcoholic personality.

After years of abstinence from alcohol, the member may feel on a plateau which, though not as disturbing as earlier plateaus, may still be fraught with anxiety. This is common, even with normal people, but the A.A. member can re-use the fourth and fifth Steps to attain an even higher and more comfortable level of mental health. When we admit to God, to ourselves and to another person, the symptoms of inner disorder, we have cast our lot with sanity. This act which is always ego-deflating, sometimes humiliating, usually very difficult, has a priceless reward: the beginning of freedom—freedom from those symptoms of mental disorder that made our lives tensely and uncomfortably sober, or destructively drunk.

Having taken these two steps (the fourth and fifth) we do not lose these defects in our personality, but now that they are out where we can see them, they are not so formidable, they lose their potency, and we are no longer in bondage to them. Remember, we were not sick because we drank, but we drank because we were sick. When we ventilate our defects, our problems, and concerns, we "talk out" much of the harmful effects of our symptoms and so we continue to get better. Occasionally a person who comes to A.A. finds that additional psychiatric help is needed to contend with deep, disturbing conflicts which may not yield to the measures in the Steps of the A.A. program alone. Psychiatry has been helpful and sympathetic to A.A. since its beginning, and any member who may benefit from this source of help in living the A.A. program should seek it.

By the time we have reached this point in our efforts, we have found and inspected much of our inner disorder. We have written down and exposed this part of ourselves to God and to another human being. Although this is necessary for recovery, and I, as a physician, do not think any alcoholic really recovers who does not take these measures, something more must occur to restore the alcoholic to sanity. One must beg God to remove these defects or manifestations of insanity. God's response to this humble appeal of the hopeless alcoholic determines whether recovery takes place. God must be especially generous with alcoholics, as witness the thousands and thousands of re-covering A.A. members who are living their daily twenty-four hours of sanity.

Experience has taught us, though, that we never reach a point of recovery where we may indulge in social drinking. Probably this is because of the special combination of traits which constitute the alcoholic personality. Also, for as long as we live, there lies within our personalities the "soil for addiction."

As day follows day, and as life goes on, the relationship with God grows, first on an emotional and warmly pleasant level, but gradually to an intellectual awareness, less glowingly sen-sual but more real. Every successful member (and all who try and pray to succeed will be successful) experiences a personal encounter with God as we know Him. Somehow, each of us know that this relationship is the basis of our recovery, and this relationship can be broken by a deliberate violation of God's Will for us. A rupture of this relationship to God leads to a sense of deep loss. The alcoholic cannot endure this loss for long.

Recovery, then has a spiritual basis. Even though the tools of psychiatry were necessary for recovery in depth, as we use them in the fourth and fifth Steps, they are not, in themselves, sufficient. The development of a spiritual life, that is, a life which is God-oriented, constitutes that which we know as "living the A.A. program."

Long term sobriety is a daily affair. Recovery, even for the person who has been living the A.A. way of life for many years, must be carefully tended. A permanent awareness of the possibility of relapse into drinking must be kept in mind. No alcoholic reaches the stage of recovery where the disturbing personality traits are dead. They may be compared to a snake which lays back in a dark corner of the mind, and which, every now and then, opens one eye to see if the alcoholic is still on guard. Being on guard consists in maintaining a life-long participation in A.A. All too frequently, we learn of a member who, after fifteen or twenty years of sobriety, returns to drinking. Invariably this person is one who has gradually drifted away from A.A. activity. The drinking is soon more destructive than when the member originally joined A.A. Frequently, the person seems unable to recapture the A.A. way of life, and dies an alcoholic death. For the large majority of members who do persist in enjoying the gift of sobriety through life-long membership in A.A., there gradually emerges a new set of attitudes. Although occasionally depressed, they are no longer afraid of this depression. Experience has taught them that these things pass. A kind of relaxed, unselfconscious life, without the violent mood swings, comes as time goes on. The ability, absolutely impossible at first, to laugh at one's self occasionally, will finally belong to the "old timer." The enjoyment of doing our jobs well, the sense of satisfaction when we know people consider us dependable, the wonderful feeling we get when our children look at us with love in their eyes—these things replace "feeling high" on a few drinks. Life, however, is not just one ecstatically happy day after another for the recovering alcoholic. Troubles affect us as they do all other humans, but our response is rational. We can face problems, we don't have to charge or flee. Turmoil may boil around us, tragedy may strike, but within our souls there is a core of peace. Our reference point is the A.A. program, our dependence is upon God.

Courtesy Robert Morse

ROBERT M. MORSE, M.D.
Chemical Dependency and Illnesses of the Mind

Dr. Robert Morse, former director of the Mayo Addiction Services in Rochester, Minnesota, contributed greatly to the development of the Minnesota Model by broadening the scope of the multidisciplinary team to better address the range of medical and psychiatric treatment that those in recovery often need. Morse realized it was not enough to limit treatment to those social, psychological, and medical issues that resulted primarily from chemical dependency. Physical, mental, and emotional issues unrelated to chemical dependency often accompanied patients into a rehabilitation program, and these conditions needed to be diagnosed and treated for successful, long-term recovery from substance abuse. In dealing with these issues of dual disorders, Morse broadened the notion of how to treat the whole person. From its inception, the Mayo program offered treatment that was truly wholistic.

Early Years
Robert Morse was born on May 21, 1934, in International Falls, Minnesota, about two blocks from the Canadian border. He speaks of his younger days as an "ideal boyhood," having been raised in a loving and caring family. His father, Harold, was in the clothing business and his mother, Lucille (Brookes), stayed at home to care for and raise him, the oldest, and his three sisters (Pamela, Patricia,

and Mary) and one brother (Thomas). While neither his mother nor father went to college, three of his four siblings were college graduates.

Morse did very well in school. Besides being an Eagle Scout, he excelled in sports and was captain of the football team. He found an outlet for his musical talent in the drums, which he played in the school band. He was called "squint" because of the way his eyes contracted with his broad smile. His memories of International Falls, of his family and upbringing, and of his education remain warm and positive. He was very active in the Congregational Church out of a sense of duty and religiosity, but as he now recalls it wasn't all that much fun.

College and Medical School

Morse was filled with an adolescent confidence that he could do anything that he set his mind to. His manifest destiny was to do something important with his life. While growing up he was always looking for challenges, which he equated with taking on the most difficult thing to do. Having finished high school, he felt that his biggest challenge would be to go to a large campus in a metropolis away from the security of family and hometown. He settled on the University of Minnesota in Minneapolis. He was good enough to play freshman football, but in his sophomore year he had to drop out when college football went from a two- to a one-platoon system, and he wasn't very good on defense.

Confronted with a lot of choices and still uncertain about what he really wanted to do as the future unfolded, Morse pursued coursework in business, law, and psychology. The one thing he was certain of was that he did not want to study science—especially biology. He finally decided to major in psychology, and after four years he graduated with a bachelor of arts degree in 1956. Two factors pushed Morse into medicine. First, Dr. Elliott, his advisor and the head of the psychology department at the university, counseled Morse in that direction. Forward in his thinking, Elliot believed that, in the future, treating patients with psychological problems would require a knowledge of the role and function that the brain plays in human behavior. Second, challenge once again beckoned

Morse, but this time it was especially difficult because he would have to study the sciences. He registered for the required premedical courses, passed them, and was accepted by the University of Minnesota College of Medicine. Four years later, in 1960, Morse obtained a bachelor of science and doctor of medicine degree.

While in his third year of medical school, Morse married Ancy Tone, a childhood friend, also from International Falls. She was in her last year of law school, and they both recall the severe time constraints at the time of their marriage. He was late for the wedding rehearsal on Friday night in International Falls because he had to take a final exam that Friday morning. They were married on Saturday, honeymooned in Duluth on Sunday, and were back in the Twin Cities for jobs on Monday.

Career

After an internship at the San Joaquin General Hospital in Stockton, California, Morse joined the air force, serving as a medical officer from 1961 until 1963 at March Air Force Base in California. The pace was hectic. The commanding officer, more demanding than managed care gatekeepers today, required the medical staff to see six patients every hour and also respond to whatever emergency occurred. At this time Morse became very interested in the emotional needs of his patients. In those days there was a decided emphasis on psychosomatic disorders, which became of great interest to him.

When he was discharged from the air force, Morse returned to Minnesota and contacted Richard McGraw, the assistant dean of the University of Minnesota Medical School. A specialist in both internal medicine and psychiatry, McGraw suggested that Morse, given his renewed interests in behavior and psychology, consider going to Mayo. With a recommendation from McGraw, Morse was able to obtain a residency as a fellow in psychiatry at the Mayo Graduate School of Medicine. In 1971 he earned a master of science degree in psychiatry from the University of Minnesota.

One of the conditions attached to the fellowship Morse had during his psychiatric training was that, upon completion of his degree, he work two years for the state. He took the opportunity to stay in the Rochester area and was assigned to the Zumbro Valley Mental Health Center as medical director. During his residency, Morse had never seriously considered the study and practice of addiction medicine. During his two years at Zumbro, however, he gained an introduction to the world of chemical dependency.

Education on the Illness of Alcoholism

Zumbro had an alcohol information center staffed by two counselors. Shortly after Morse arrived, a few board members at the mental health center suggested that he consider the possibility of starting an outpatient treatment facility for alcoholics. Morse was reluctant at first, given his lack of knowledge and practical experience. He knew very little about addiction and even less about alcoholism. An alcohol information counselor named Ray Island, who knew what alcoholism was all about and what alcoholics needed, took Morse under his wing and provided him with an informal education. Island introduced Morse to the disease concept of alcoholism, the reality of powerlessness and the importance of the First Step of AA. Island also taught him about the manifold ways that alcoholics had of expressing their denial about their drinking and its consequences. (Later the two of them made a tape for the patients in which Island acted out the denial patterns. Nicknamed the "Ray and Bob Show," it became a very effective tool in treating the patients, who would watch the video and without fail see themselves mirrored in some phase of it. Island had covered every conceivable form of denial.)

Still, Morse had difficulty with the idea that alcoholism could be a disease. Island would bring him to open AA meetings, taking some pride in being able to introduce his "psychiatrist" friend to other recovering people. Morse wasn't always comfortable with Island's missionary effort, but he was grateful for the experience and the firsthand knowledge that would otherwise be missing from his education. He witnessed how alcoholics welcomed to their meetings anyone with the desire to get help, no matter what their past behavior was. Acceptance was a fundamental spiritual principle. Morse was also really impressed by that aspect of the program that taught alcoholics to learn how to forgive themselves. Island introduced

Morse to the Reverend Phil Hansen, who would become a prominent figure in the history of alcoholism and its treatment in Minnesota. Morse was impressed with the clergyman's talks and with the
reactions of others who felt that Hansen "saw more Christianity in
AA than in the Church itself."

The major thing that Morse had to unlearn was that "addiction
was nothing but a symptom of another underlying problem," in
other words, psychodynamically rooted. In his professional dealings
with alcoholics, he began to wonder why he could not discover the
other problem. Was he just too stupid? And if it were difficult for
him, he thought, how hard it must be for other doctors, since he at
least had some understanding of the alcoholics' behavior.

Gradually Morse put together a modest continuum of care for
alcoholics at the Zumbro Center, which basically consisted of formal assessments of the patients who enrolled, one-on-ones with
counselors, and the opportunity to participate in group therapy. For
patients in need of detoxication, Morse used the detox unit at the
Olmsted Community Hospital. There, he re-united with a medical-
school classmate, Jim Garber, who helped educate him about the
nature of alcoholism. Garber later became the medical director at
Guest House in Rochester, a treatment facility for Roman Catholic
priests. There was no detox unit at Mayo. If you were an "alcoholic"
you were put into the locked psychiatric ward at St. Mary's Hospital. At that time Mayo continued the misunderstanding that alcoholics were prone to violence and had to be carefully watched at
all times.

In 1967, while still at Zumbro, Morse initiated a weekly alcoholism group for men. He moved the group to Mayo when he took a
position there the following year. As of 2001, the group had been
running continuously for thirty-four years and had retained a
strong contingent of recovering alcoholics. Hearing people tell their
stories, observing their lifestyle changes, and noting their relapses
and responses to traumatic experiences, Morse observed that most
long-term recoveries came from people who were eventually grateful
for much in their lives, including being alcoholic. They learned to
be open and honest with others, and many of them began to appreciate that their current lives were better than they possibly would

have been had they not discovered and recovered from their alcoholism. Morse likes to refer to these people as "weller than well" because of their added dimension of gratitude.

Treating alcoholics and working with the recovering counselors and chaplains on multidisciplinary teams increased Morse's personal interest in philosophy and spirituality. He defines his own spiritual journey as a relentless pursuit for the meaning of life. As part of that spiritual journey, he continues to read widely in the areas of Christian, Buddhist, and Native American spirituality. Ralph Waldo Emerson holds a special attraction for him.

The Influence of Other Professionals

Besides the informal education and indoctrination Morse received from Island, he found other professionals from different quarters to be especially encouraging. In 1967 he attended a seminar at Mayo put on by Dan Anderson from Hazelden, Dick Heilman from the Veteran's Hospital in Minneapolis, and the Reverend Phil Hansen from Abbott Northwestern in Minneapolis. Morse was impressed both with the people presenting and with their message about how treatment could help people get well. While introducing the panel to the Mayo audience, Dr. Richard Steinhilber, chair of Mayo's department of psychiatry, said: "I believe that from this session we will get a better idea of how medicine is going to change and how all diseases are going to have to be approached in a multidiscipline level if we are to come to better grips with understanding the cause of the disease as well as with the concept of treating the whole person."

In 1969 Morse joined the American Medical Society on Alcoholism (AMSA), whose president at the time was Ruth Fox. He wrote to her inquiring about the use of Antabuse, a drug given to alcoholics (with their consent) to make them ill if they imbibe any more alcohol. Fox sent Morse a long letter assuring him of the drug's safety and its results in helping alcoholics stay sober—results she herself observed in her own clinical practice. AMSA met annually after the meeting of the National Council on Alcoholism. Doctors interested in the disease of alcoholism and its treatment were in attendance. Morse remembers meeting, among others, Enoch Gordis, Frank Seixas, Maxwell Weisman, Stan Gitlow, and

Nelson Bradley. They all assured him that he was moving in the right direction, that alcoholism was something really distinct in itself and not secondary to some other psychiatric disorder.

Morse began to visit a number of people at their various residential programs: Dan Anderson at Hazelden, Vern Johnson at St. Mary's Hospital, Phil Hansen at Abbott Northwestern, Dick Heilman at the Veteran's Hospital in Minneapolis, and Nelson Bradley at Lutheran General in Chicago. The more he traveled and visited, the more he became wedded to the disease concept of alcoholism.

Nelson Bradley, one of the founders of the Minnesota Model, was especially helpful. He had been the superintendent of Willmar State Hospital in the 1950s, before being hired to replicate the Minnesota Model at Lutheran General Hospital in Chicago. At Willmar, Bradley had implemented a program that represented a radical departure from the conventional understanding of alcoholism as a psychiatric condition. He had separated the alcoholics from the mentally ill, left their doors unlocked, and allowed AA members to talk with the patients.

What Morse particularly admired about Bradley was that, for a psychiatrist, he seemed unusually open to the opinions of other professionals. Bradley approached some of the more disturbed alcoholics as though they had two illnesses: alcoholism and a psychiatric disorder. Besides their interest in the treatment of alcoholics, Bradley and Morse had another thing in common—zoology. Wherever they met at conferences they would spend some time together at the local zoo searching out the more exotic animals.

Dan Anderson and his staff, particularly Dick Heilman, the consulting psychiatrist at Hazelden, and Dee Smith, the head nurse, were most helpful when Morse began conceptualizing and implementing a program at Mayo. From Hazelden, Morse learned practical methods of detoxication as well as the latest developments in the Minnesota Model of treatment.

Nils Bejerot, Swedish Scientist

Morse also began to read extensively about alcoholism and rehabilitation: in particular, the Big Book, the writings by the psychiatrist

Harry Tiebout on the psychopathology of denial and the role the ego plays in alcoholism, *The New Primer on Alcoholism* by Marty Mann, and the *Afflicted and the Affected* by Phil Hansen. Morse kept current with all the material that was being published by Hazelden. What influenced him the most was a paper delivered by a Swedish scientist, Nils Bejerot, before an international audience in 1970.

Bejerot had concluded from his studies that neither intrinsic personality disorders nor external social problems were to blame for a person's becoming dependent upon alcohol or drugs. He believed that any individual could develop an addiction if certain substances were administered in certain quantities during a certain period of time. These chemicals affect the nervous system and provide such pleasure that the individual finds it difficult to do without. After indulging in this pleasure for a period of time, the person finds it almost impossible to surrender the use of the chemical. Bejerot's conclusion: "This dependence has developed the character and strength of a basic drive—the craving or hunger for the drug has developed into a need which may be as strong or even stronger than a sexual desire. The use or abuse of drugs has developed into a severe illness, addiction, and the drug abuser has become a severe addict."[1]

This conclusion was what Morse had been looking for—a scientific construct to explain the nature, the "why" of alcoholism. He had found the allergy hypothesis in the Big Book wanting. Bejerot's basic drive theory was much more appealing to his scientific mind. Somehow it seemed to him to add strength to the practical experience of AA.

Bejerot addressed the unmanageability and powerlessness that the individual experiences. Contrary to natural drives, the artificially induced drives tend to bring about a deterioration of individual adaptation and social functioning, which he described as "social insufficiency." Loss of control and powerlessness over drug consumption occur when the drug addiction has been established and craving controls the addict's way of life. The individual's normal free will is put out of action. "Willpower and desires often collide in everyday life, and we need not be psychologically disturbed or weak-willed individuals to be unable to master our drives."[2] Denial is described as a natural defense mechanism to protect basic drives. The addict's deception and unreliability are to be seen in light of this denial.

While there is no mention of AA in Bejerot's tract, there is an extraordinarily similar parallel between his thinking about treatment and care for the chemically dependent and the development of the continuum of care in the Minnesota Model. He wrote of the need for long-term care for the addicts. He indicated, already in 1972, that general agreement exists on a need for a number of small, closed psychiatric wards for the initial phases of treatment—detoxication and diagnoses. Six months of treatment would then be required, either at the psychiatric hospital or at another place removed from the old milieu in which the addiction was practiced.

Aftercare played an important role in Bejerot's vision. Relapse of various degrees of severity was a constant threat and usually occurred when the patient met old "using" friends. New friends and different environments were essential to recovery. Patients had little chance of recovery when they departed treatment without a job, a place to live, occupational advice, psychotherapy, and group activity. An essential component in recovery, then, was an aftercare home that was guided and mentored by competent staff that possessed a real knowledge of the problem. Bejerot referred to the trilogy of education, information, and prevention as a form of vaccination against this illness of addiction.

Morse also noted with import that Bejerot addressed the issue of dual diagnosis and warned that many addicts had severe personality disorders long before becoming addicted. Expectations therefore had to be realistic. Addiction treatment would not succeed in "curing" all addicts by returning them to "normal" life.

The Alcohol and Drug Dependency Unit at Mayo

Besides providing Morse with a scientific construct to help him understand the nature of alcoholism, Bejerot's concepts came at a particularly propitious time for Morse, who was formulating his own ideas for a treatment unit at Mayo. In 1968 he had been appointed a consultant in psychiatry at the Mayo Clinic, a position he held until he retired in 2000. He also continued to consult at the Zumbro outpatient clinic until 1972. His experiences at Zumbro made him more and more interested in establishing a residential treatment program at Mayo, where he found that anyone diagnosed as alcoholic was locked in a psychiatric ward. Furthermore, doctors usually ended up euphemizing alcoholism by concealing it under some other diagnosis, so Morse really had no idea how much need there might be for a facility at Mayo. Most of his colleagues at Mayo with whom he talked about a center showed little or no interest.

Nevertheless, Morse's experience with Zumbro's outpatient program told him that the need for a residential rehabilitation center was great. Fortunately, his persistence won the attention of Steinhilber, who had already shown some interest in the issue of alcoholism by inviting Anderson, Heilman, and Hansen to present a seminar at Mayo in 1967. In 1970 Steinhilber gave Morse the green light to start a program.

As the opening day approached, Morse sent the nurses and counselors that he had hired to Hazelden for some further training. The program he was installing was based on Hazelden's Minnesota Model, but with more intensive medical and psychiatric components capable of dealing with problems diagnosed in those areas.

The Alcohol and Drug Dependency Unit at Mayo opened as a twenty-four-bed residential unit in March 1972, in the Old Colonial

The Generose Building, where the Mayo Addiction Services, initially instituted by Dr. Robert Morse, now resides. Courtesy Robert Morse

building off the east edge of Rochester Methodist Hospital. Ten years later the center relocated to the ninth floor of Methodist Hospital. In 1993 it moved to its current location, on St. Mary's campus in the Generose Building, and is now called the Mayo Addiction Services.

On opening day of the Alcoholism and Drug Dependency Unit, a full complement of staff—including Ray Island, whom Morse had hired from Zumbro—assembled with a program that included daily lectures and two groups a day. But with only three patients, Morse wondered what the future held and whether treatment would work with so few patients. It did and he persevered. Half the beds were filled at the end of the first year, and by the end of the second year there was a waiting list of patients to get into the facility.

Professional Counselors and Psychiatrists in Residence

From the start the therapy groups were led jointly by a professional counselor trained in chemical dependency and a physician who was also a resident in psychiatry. The presence of the physician guaranteed both consistent medical care and a psychiatric perspective for the group therapy. Besides having close daily contact with the patients, the physicians were able to interact with and learn from the recovering counselors during the group sessions. The counselors and the physicians gradually became more comfortable with one another as they shared thoughts, ideas, and experiences. As Morse later reflected: "This physician-counselor model has become the core of our treatment team as well as the most effective educational experience for young psychiatrists."[3]

The psychiatrists were able to handle the "crazy" behavior that patients sometimes manifested, whether it was due to their immediate withdrawal, to post acute withdrawal, or to the stress placed upon them in the beginning of the recovery journey. The psychiatrists were also able to address any psychiatric problems that emerged. The broad-based treatment team allowed for a wholistic approach, with a better understanding of the whole person.

Morse followed Steinhilber's example to educate the doctors at Mayo about the disease of alcoholism and its social and economic consequences nationwide. At one such event, Morse capitalized on the interest many of the professionals had in the theater. He and a social worker on his staff named Mary Martin persuaded Jason Robards, an award-winning actor noted for his portrayals of characters in plays by Eugene O'Neill, to come to Rochester to recite the famous soliloquy from O'Neill's *The Iceman Cometh,* in which a salesman reveals the many faces of denial to the drinking patrons of a bar and forces them to strip away their illusions about life and to accept death. More than a thousand people filled the Mayo auditorium. The master of ceremonies, Morse led a panel that included Robards, Dan Anderson from Hazelden, and Morse's colleague Bob Niven (who later became the director of the National Institute on Alcohol Abuse and Alcoholism). The event enhanced the prestige of the fledgling alcohol unit among the doctors on the Mayo campus.

Medicalizing the Minnesota Model

Because "crazy" behavior is often related to the abuse of drugs or to withdrawal from them, the unit at Mayo had to develop a way to deal with it. When the program first started, this meant "waiting it out" before doing a battery of diagnostic tests to determine the nature of the behavior. But the staff soon realized that the issue was more complicated; some of the patients who entered treatment did indeed have a psychiatric disorder that had become disguised by the alcoholic disorder. With its medical resources, Mayo was able to offer concurrent treatment of dual diagnosis patients at the Alcohol and Drug Dependency Unit.

Morse describes his program as one that "medicalizes" the Minnesota Model by tending to the physical and psychological stability of patients. To ensure physical stability, every patient has a comprehensive general medical examination and can obtain specialist or surgical consultation as needed. When feasible, Mayo provides other medical treatment while patients remain hospitalized for chemical dependency care. For example, treatment of hypertension, rheumatoid arthritis, or diabetes mellitus is easily managed within the rehabilitation unit.

To ensure psychological stability, each patient has a formal psychiatric interview and evaluation as part of the standard admissions workup. The program can then treat any number of psychiatric disorders simultaneously with addiction. At Mayo it is common "to actively treat nonpsychotic psychiatric disorders or evaluate patients for these disorders as they progress through the various phases of intoxication, withdrawal, and abstinence." Because the program environment at Mayo "is highly structured, with tightly scheduled activities and specific rules and regulations," Morse feels that it can be therapeutic especially for character pathology or personality disorders. The program contains "specific prohibitions against acting-out behaviors. Regressive behavior is discouraged, while coping skills are encouraged. Patients are asked to recognize uncomfortable and previously unacceptable feelings and thoughts, to tolerate them, and also to similarly tolerate difficult behavior in their peers. They must begin to tolerate frustration, control their impulses, and regulate their feelings. Such a milieu is probably the best available treatment approach for the inflexible and maladaptive behavior patterns classified as 'personality disorders.'"[4]

This medicalized treatment model can be adapted to the particular needs of various populations, such as physicians, chronic pain patients, and the elderly. Many chronic pain patients become addicted to their prescribed medications. In the Mayo program these patients recovered at the same rate as other addicts, and physicians with addiction had a better prognosis than patients in general.

In an article entitled "Substance Abuse Among the Elderly," Morse reviewed the prevalence of substance abuse among this population and considered the biological and pharmacological factors: the variety of symptoms that the elderly present, their biological sensitivity to chemicals, and the dependency traps that they can fall into by abusing the use of alcohol, prescription drugs, or over-the-counter drugs. To counteract these factors, medical professionals and the community at large need to be informed about the scope of the drugs used by the elderly and about the treatment that can be effective for them.

When a multispecialty center like Mayo offers this medicalized version of the Minnesota Model, it can do even more than provide wholistic treatment. The program at Mayo also provides educational opportunities for nearly 1,000 staff physicians and medical scientists and another 800 resident physicians and clinical fellows.

And the psychiatrists on the multidisciplinary teams conduct research to further our knowledge of chemical dependency. Besides studies on the elderly, Morse and his colleagues have compiled research on other populations: physicians, those with nicotine dependence, and those who suffer chronic pain.

The Impact of Managed Care

Like the rest of the chemical dependency field, the Alcohol and Drug Dependence Unit at Mayo began to experience difficulties in the mid-1980s. Managed care organizations began to require drastic changes among the treatment networks. As Morse noted, programs were "being asked to care for patients with more complex problems with shorter stays, fewer staff, reduced costs, increased efficiency, improved outcomes, and greater patient satisfaction—clearly an impossible dream."[5]

The influence of managed care led to a great increase in outpatient services. Most of the program's patients are now handled on an outpatient basis, but Mayo offers three options for chemical dependency treatment:

1. The inpatient program is geared toward severe cases of alcoholism and other addictions. These are patients who, along with the chemical dependency, usually present other problems that need medical attention.
2. Partial hospitalization is designed for patients who do not need to stay in the hospital the whole day and who usually go home in the evening after attending group sessions during the day.
3. The outpatient program is for those who can still carry on in their daily lives of work, family, etc. Patients can enroll either for an intensive fifteen hours a week for three weeks or for less intensive group therapy on a weekly basis.

Writing about the impact of managed care on treatment, Morse observed: "When efforts began a few years ago to reduce the tendency to place alcoholics in four-week residential programs whether or not it was clinically indicated, we agreed that some abuses should be avoided. At the same time, however, we were reassured that seriously ill and complex patients with high degrees of comorbidity would be granted longer lengths of stay as treatment programs were more 'individualized.' This ideal has not materialized. We have yet to see even a four-week stay granted through managed care."[6]

The last word on managed care has yet to be written, but there is no doubt that it has inflicted severe damage on the continuum of care that seeks to serve those afflicted with chemical dependency. Nor has this damage been limited to inpatient treatment. For out-patient programs, as well, money dictates the nature and length of treatment.

Retirement

After retiring from the Mayo Clinic in 2000, Morse began to reflect on his career. He talks fondly of his colleagues and his association with the Mayo Clinic. Being affiliated with Mayo has been a source of pride. "People trust you, even envy you, because of affiliation with the Mayo name and all of its medical talent and excellent facilities." For its part, Mayo can take pride in the unique program that Morse forged, even though he himself modestly refers to it as a "small fish in a big pond."

Testimony to Morse's success in the field of medicine are his memberships on hospital, state, and national committees; his clinical

Dr. Robert Morse and his wife, Ancy Tone. Ancy served fifteen years as a district judge and forty years in the legal profession. Courtesy Robert Morse

experience; and his addiction research projects, on which he has published more than sixty articles in various journals. Moreover, his credibility as a psychiatrist is not limited to the practice of addiction medicine. Half of his professional time was devoted to treating people with other mental disorders totally unrelated to chemical dependency. His peers have honored him with the Distinguished Mayo Clinician Award (the first bestowed in the department of psychiatry) and with the status of full professor at the Mayo Medical School.

But Morse takes even more pride in his family. He and his wife Ancy, who retired after fifteen years as a district judge and forty years in the legal profession, have three daughters and one son. Kathy and Karen have studied and worked in the field of social services before becoming full-time mothers. Kelly is still uncertain of her vocational journey after having majored in religion at the University of Chicago. Mark, the youngest, has an MBA but shares his father's love for music and percussion instruments.

Occasionally Robert Morse can be found playing the drums with a big band, the Notochords in Rochester. His staid colleagues at the clinic, accustomed to his outstanding performance as director of the Mayo Addiction Services and as staff psychiatrist, are usually surprised to see him there and discover how well he plays. For some of them, it may appear incongruous for a serious and successful psychiatrist to be equally talented as a musician, playing drums for fun with his pixie-like smile. Likewise, for recovering people it may have appeared incongruous for a nonrecovering psychiatrist to be so successful and popular orchestrating the dissonant and multifaceted chords of chemical dependency.

Notes

1.   Nils Bejerot, *Addiction—An Artificially Induced Drive* (Springfield, Ill.: Charles C. Thomas: 1972), 3.
2.   Ibid., 7.
3.   Robert M. Morse, M.D., "Medicalizing the Minnesota Model," *Professional Counselor* (August 1991): 33.
4.   Ibid., 35.
5.   Robert M. Morse, M.D., "The Uneasy Alliance Between Managed Care and Clinical Services," *Front Lines* (October 1995): 1.
6.   Ibid., 2.

Medicalizing the Minnesota Model
BY ROBERT M. MORSE, MD

With its reputation for leadership in working with alcoholics and other chemically dependent people, Minnesota has been nicknamed by a recent publication[1] "land of 10,000 recovery programs"—a takeoff on its official nickname, "Land of 10,000 Lakes."

Spawning many well-known treatment institutions and other organizations in the addictions field, the state is perhaps best known for the "Minnesota Model" of treatment. This was spearheaded by psychiatrist Nelson Bradley and psychologist Dan Anderson at Willmar State Hospital about 1950.[2] Introducing the revolutionary concept that alcoholism was a primary illness that could be treated directly and behaviorally, irrespective of the initial motivation for treatment, these innovators brought the Twelve Step philosophy of AA into their "therapeutic community" concept. The latter seemed to provide a separate community for chemically dependent patients, where the total environment would be therapeutic and could be controlled to enhance behavioral change over a "relatively short time" (then 60 days).[2]

Since then, the Minnesota Model has influenced the residential care of chemically dependent persons throughout the world. Although there is occasional disagreement about the actual components of this model, the following are usually listed: group therapy, use of recovering lay counselors, lectures, multiprofessional staff, therapeutic milieu, work assignments, family involvement, a Twelve Step (AA) program, daily readings from AA literature, AA attendance, and recreation.[3]

When the decision was made to open the Alcoholism and Drug Dependence Unit (ADDU) at Mayo Clinic in 1972, we searched for an appropriate treatment model that would provide

Originally published in Professional Counselor, *August 1991, 33–35. Reprinted with permission from Health Communications, Inc.*

the best therapeutic experience for our patients and that would meet the other two goals of our institution: to provide educational opportunities for medical students and young physicians, and to contribute by research to the advancement of knowledge. Clearly the Minnesota Model seemed to provide the best residential treatment experience. It did not, however, seem to provide the ongoing medical or scientific influence required for a program that would become the focal point of both teaching and treating addictive disorders in a large tertiary-care medical center with more than 1,800 hospital beds, 900-plus staff physicians and medical scientists, and more than 800 resident physicians and clinical fellows. The model would have to be more "medicalized" to serve this function.

Perusal of existing literature, site visits to several respected treatment centers, and ongoing multilevel staff discussions eventually allowed us to develop a modification of the Minnesota Model that, although always evolving and changing, has for the most part met the challenges set before us. In addition to the therapeutic milieu components already listed as typifying the Minnesota Model program, our medicalized version also includes the following:

1. Integration of our psychiatric residency training program with staffing needs of the treatment unit. This allows for on-site, full-time assignment of physicians to the treatment team (currently three resident physicians for a bed capacity of 33 patients).
2. Assignment of experienced staff psychiatrists with interest in the addictions field to a daily supervisory capacity (two consultant psychiatrists at any one time). This psychiatric staffing allows each patient to have a formal psychiatric interview and evaluation as part of the standard admission workup.
3. A comprehensive general medical examination for each patient on admission, supervised by a consultant staff internist.
4. Special medical or surgical consultation as required—done

much as they would be on any other hospital unit by having consulting physicians visit patients at the ADDU.

5. Provision, when feasible, of medical treatment while patients remain hospitalized for chemical dependency care. For example, treatment of peptic ulcer disease, hypertension, rheumatoid arthritis, and diabetes mellitus are easily managed in the ADDU by this model.

6. Concurrent psychiatric treatment of "dual diagnosis" patients at the ADDU. This will be discussed further.

7. Assignment of resident physicians and counselors as coleaders of treatment teams (three teams of 11 patients on the 33-bed unit). This serves many purposes. It provides regular and consistent medical care for patients and a psychiatric perspective to the twice-a-day group therapy meetings. It offers an excellent learning opportunity for physicians who are in close daily contact not only with their patients, but also with "recovering counselors" with whom they can interact and learn. Furthermore, there is a cross-fertilization of ideas and roles as counselors and physicians become more comfortable with one another and share thoughts, ideas, and experiences. This physician-counselor model has become the core of our treatment team as well as the most effective educational experience for young psychiatrists.

An early and ongoing concern was our worry that the medicalized Minnesota Model, which encouraged open and critical discussion of the state of knowledge and treatment approaches, might provide [sic] too threatening to attract well-trained counselors, whose educational experiences had generally been spent at nonmedical institutions. This could not have been further from the truth!

After an initial settling-in period, most of our counselors (currently there are seven) rapidly adapted to the system and enjoyed their shoulder-to-shoulder relationships with physicians. Comments from current counselors give us a flavor of their impressions: "It's an opportunity to provide better overall care, and it's very stimulating—always some new ideas to consider!" Or, "You become more confident in the overall treatment approach after a comprehensive evaluation and more sure that you know what you are dealing with. You feel that you can push patients more to their limits, not fearing that you are going too far. Working alone in the community or as the only professional available, I used to worry a lot that maybe I had missed something in addition to the chemical dependency." And, "There is a mutual respect between the professions. You can overcome professional boundaries, and you are constantly learning from each other." Finally, "Not everything can be blamed on chemical dependency, and with our broad-based treatment team, we are in a position to try to better understand the whole person."

Within the model discussed, it is commonplace to treat any number of psychiatric disorders simultaneously with addiction. The chief limiting factor in our milieu is the overt behavior of patients. For example, frankly and floridly psychotic (e.g., schizophrenic or manic) patients may need transfer to the psychiatric unit for more structured and controlled psychiatric management. However, if the schizophrenia is in remission, which usually means that a patient is being actively treated with a neuroleptic drug, we have found that patient to be just as likely as any other to absorb the cognitive and educational aspects of the treatment milieu. Emotional response may be more blunted than in others, but this does not necessarily inhibit satisfactory treatment progress.[4]

It is much more common, however, for us to actively treat nonpsychotic psychiatric disorders or evaluate patients for these disorders as they progress through the various phases of intoxication, withdrawal, and abstinence. At the writing of this article, the following psychiatric patients were being evaluated and treated on our Alcoholism and Drug Dependence Unit:

A 53-year-old woman with a previous psychiatric diagnosis of generalized anxiety disorder initially treated with Xanax (alprazolam), who later became dependent upon the prescription drug Klonopin (clonazepam). She has just been carefully detoxified from clonazepam with some minor anxiety symptoms. Our eventual challenge is to determine whether she has an anxiety disorder in addition to her addictive disorder, and if so, to determine the best treatment approach to minimize the risk of her returning to addicting drugs.

A 40-year-old woman addicted to Xanax, which by her report she has been taking regularly for at least eight years. She has a long history of intermittent psychiatric hospitalizations for "borderline personality disorder" and is a difficult management problem with staff manipulations, multiple somatic complaints, and several psychiatric symptoms to deal with in addition to the withdrawal regimen.

A 19-year-old unmarried woman, probably schizophrenic (although the diagnosis is a bit obscure), taking a moderate dose of a neuroleptic medication to control her psychotic symptoms. She was transferred to our facility after her behavior worsened during a long hospitalization in another psychiatric facility. She clearly has an addictive syndrome and has impulsively ingested drugs and nonbeverage alcohol whenever available. At present, she has little interest, insight, or motivation for treatment.

A 65-year-old woman currently being detoxified from another prescription benzodiazepine tranquilizer (Ativan) that she became dependent upon while being treated for serious depression. She is also taking antidepressant medication, which we will taper soon since we are not certain whether it may be contributing to her rather unusual mental status, which includes pressured and tangential speech.

This treatment model has also allowed us to provide treatment emphasis for such special populations as addicted physicians,[5] chronic pain patients,[6] and the elderly.[7]

We believe that a well-run therapeutic milieu in a residential substance abuse program with the Minnesota Model, as just described, can also be therapeutic for other types of psychopathology, especially character pathology or personality disorder. As discussed by Nace,[8] this environment is highly structured, with tightly scheduled activities and specific rules and regulations. Limit setting is overt and constant, with specific prohibitions against acting-out behaviors. Regressive behavior is discouraged, coping skills are encouraged, and self-care with some independent living is required. Patients are asked to recognize uncomfortable and previously unacceptable feelings and thoughts, to tolerate them, and also to similarly tolerate difficult behavior in their peers. They must begin to tolerate frustration, control their impulses, and regulate their feelings.

Such a milieu is probably the best available treatment approach for the inflexible and maladaptive behavior patterns classified as "personality disorders."

We believe that not only can other psychiatric disorders be managed effectively on a Minnesota Model treatment unit, but that the entire milieu has practical and theoretical psychotherapeutic value. Involving onsite medical-psychiatric personnel with substance abuse counselors and a sophisticated staff of other professionals (nurses, chaplain, social worker, recreational therapist, biofeedback therapist) allows the process to blossom more formally into a truly therapeutic environment.

References

1. *U.S. Journal of Drug and Alcohol Dependence,* Volume 6(2), February 1991.
2. Anderson, Daniel J. "Perspectives on Treatment." Hazelden Foundation, 1981.
3. Curson, David A. "Private Treatment of Alcohol and Drug Problems in Britain." *British Journal of Addiction,* 1991, 86:9–11.
4. Morse, Robert M. "Schizophrenia and Alcoholism." (Letter) *JAMA,* 1985, 253:3606.

5. Morse, R.M.; Martin, M.A.; Swenson W.M.; and Niven R.G. "Prognosis of Physicians Treated for Alcoholism and Drug Dependence." *JAMA,* 1984, 251:743–746.

6. Finlayson, R.E.; Maruta, T.; Morse, R.M.; and Martin, M.A. "Substance Dependence in Chronic Pain: Experience with Treatment and Follow-Up Results." *PAIN,* 1986, 26:175–180.

7. Hurt, R.D.; Finlayson, R.E.; Morse, R.M.; and Davis, L.J. "Alcoholism in Elderly Persons: Medical Aspects and Prognosis of 216 Patients." Mayo Clinic Proceedings, 1988, 63:753–760.

8. Nace, Edgar P. "Substance Abuse and Personality Disorder," in O'Connell, David F., Editor: *Managing the Dually Diagnosed Patient.* The Haworth Press Inc., New York, 1990.

Prognosis of Physicians Treated for Alcoholism and Drug Dependence

ROBERT M. MORSE, MD; MARY A. MARTIN; WENDELL M. SWENSON, PHD; ROBERT G. NIVEN, MD

Data on 73 physicians are compared with data on 185 middle-class patients similarly treated for alcoholism or drug dependence in a hospital-based inpatient program. General patients were contacted one year after treatment and physicians, one to five years later. The prognosis was more favorable for physicians than for general patients. When the groups were selected for study on the basis of completion of inpatient treatment, availability at time of contact, and not having died, 83% of physicians and 62% of the general group were noted to have favorable outcomes. Close monitoring may account, in part, for the better prognosis for physicians.

(*JAMA* 1984; 251:743–746)

During the past decade, much attention has been drawn to the problem of recognizing and rehabilitating the impaired or "sick" physician.[1] General agreement exists that alcoholism and other drug dependence (addictive disorders) are major health hazards to physicians. An earlier Mayo Clinic study of 93 physicians admitted to a psychiatric ward noted that more than half were alcoholic or drug dependent.[2] Since the opening of the Alcoholism and Drug Dependence Unit at the Mayo Clinic, Rochester, Minn, in 1972, at least 5% of new admissions for the ensuing five years involved physicians. This was the largest specific occupational group treated. Therefore, there is evidence that addiction may be the primary behavioral condition for which physicians are hospitalized, and, in a middle-class population hospitalized for treatment of that disorder, physicians are the preponderant profession.

It has been suggested that, because of these and other experi-

Originally published in Journal of the American Medical Association (JAMA) *251, no. 6 (10 February 1984): 743–746. Copyrighted 1984, American Medical Association. Reprinted with permission.*

ences, physicians are more vulnerable to alcoholism and drug dependence than the general population. We are unaware of reliable incidence or prevalence studies documenting this. Although the rate of alcoholism among physicians has not been established, a recent Mayo Clinic study showed that 7% of physicians surveyed were possible or probable alcoholics, a percentage almost identical to that of similarly surveyed general medical outpatients.[3,4] This rate is consistent with figures quoted by federal authorities for the population in general.[5]

Drug use and the abuse of prescription drugs does seem to be more prevalent among physicians.[6–8] Yet it is often not clear whether this is drug dependence. Physicians may enter treatment facilities or otherwise come to attention at a higher rate than do nonphysicians.

An increasing number of reports show that physicians treated for addiction have a relatively favorable prognosis. Goby et al[9] reported that 65% of alcoholic physicians followed up for a mean of 42 months either were totally abstinent or had only occasional relapses. Moreover, two thirds of addicted physicians treated at the Menninger Clinic, Topeka, Kan, were described as sober and practicing, although they may have had brief relapses nine months to 4 1/2 years after treatment.[10] Kliner et al[11] described an abstinence rate of 76% for alcoholic physicians who responded to a questionnaire one year after treatment. However, 21% of this group either had died or did not respond to the questionnaire survey. More recently, Herrington et al,[12] at the DePaul Rehabilitation Hospital, Milwaukee, reported that 67% of addicted physicians maintained abstinence during participation in a two-year program.

These studies have not attempted to compare outcome for physicians with other patients similarly treated for addiction. Although the report by Kliner et al[11] refers briefly to "76% of the physicians but only 61% of the patients in the general patient population being abstinent for 1 year after discharge,"

there is no description of how the general patients were selected, treated, or followed up.

We have had an opportunity to compare the outcomes of
treatment for addiction to alcohol and other drugs in a group of
physician patients and in a group of middle-class patients.

Methods

The study involved 73 physicians who were contacted in 1978,
an average of 37 months after the completion of treatment
(range, one through five years), and 185 general patients who
were contacted in 1975, one year after treatment. The average
age for each group was 49 years. Men made up 92% of the
physician group and 75% of the general group. Analysis of
outcome by sex difference in the general group, however, failed
to disclose obvious differences. Sixty-one (84%) of the physicians and 141 (76%) of the general group were married. The
relatively high educational level and socioeconomic status of
the general group are indicated by data from an earlier study of
867 general patients from our program, in which 23% were
college graduates and 29% were in executive or professional
occupations.[13]

The Alcoholism and Drug Dependence Unit is a 24-bed inpatient treatment program located in a large medical center
with 1,800 hospital beds. The multidisciplinary-staffed unit
has attempted to integrate accepted modalities for addiction
treatment with psychiatric and specialty-oriented medical care.
The treatment approach is based on a "disease concept" of addiction, by which it is understood that these disorders cease to
be symptoms of underlying problems once they reach the addictive stage and, therefore, must be approached as "primary
disorders." Although patients accept the nature of this primary
illness, many have associated psychiatric and medical disorders
that receive concurrent management. The duration of treatment is three to six weeks, with a four-week average stay. Pre-

liminary analysis shows no relationship between the age of the patient or the length of inpatient treatment and prognosis.

Each patient received an initial diagnostic assessment, including an internist-directed general medical examination, detailed drug and alcohol histories, psychiatric evaluation, psychological testing, and spouse or family interviews. Special medical and surgical consultations were arranged as necessary. The multimodal treatment approach included educational measures, individual and group psychotherapy, addiction counseling, physical exercise, family participation, and an introduction to AA. Detailed aftercare planning preceded dismissal from the hospital.

Patients were contacted by one of us, who was the aftercare coordinator (M.A.M.). These were generally telephone contacts, often confirmed by a third party. Forty-five (85%) of physician contacts were confirmed, usually by the spouse but occasionally by a parent, friend, physician, or pastor. A much smaller proportion of the general group were confirmed. Some contacts were personal interviews, and some follow-up information was provided by other staff members.

Of the original subjects, 44 (24%) of the general group were excluded from the study, as were 20 (27%) of the physician group because of incomplete treatment, death, or inability to be reached (Table 1). Incomplete treatment was defined as leaving the treatment program before the end of two weeks. Fewer physicians than general patients left early. The death rate of the two groups was similar, when considering that the follow-up period for the physician group was up to five years and only one year for the general group. Only three (2%) of the general group and four (5%) of the physician group could not be reached. The eventual study groups were composed of 141 (76%) of the original general group and 53 (73%) of the physician group.

Outcome categories were defined as follows: (1) abstinence

since dismissal, (2) brief relapse (no longer than one week in duration) but abstinent when contacted and no evidence of return to the addictive pattern, (3) drinking or using drugs, but improved with regard to pattern and consequences of use, and (4) no improvement in drinking or drug use.

We arbitrarily considered categories 1 and 2 as favorable and 3 and 4 as unfavorable. Although category 3 (the "controlled drinker") could be considered favorable, our experience suggests that this is not a stable or predictable state and often is the initial regression into addictive alcohol or drug use (relapse). Furthermore, complete abstinence from alcohol and other drugs of abuse is an announced treatment goal of the program. Recent studies continue to refute seriously the idea of controlled drinking as being a reasonable treatment goal for alcoholic patients.[14]

Results

Favorable outcome (categories 1 and 2) was noted for 44 (83%) of the physicians and 87 (62%) of the general group, a significant difference ($P<.01$, x^2). Four (8%) of the physicians were in outcome group 4, compared with 34 (24%) of the general group. When the entire series included patients who died, patients with incomplete treatment, and uncontacted patients, 60% of the physician group and 47% of the general group had favorable outcomes.

Table 1.

Composition of Study Groups in Treatment of Alcoholism and Drug Dependence				
	General Group		Physician Group	
	No.	%	No.	%
In study	141	76	53	73
Excluded	44	24	20	27
Treatment incomplete	37	20	7	10
Dead	4	2	9	12
Not contacted	3	2	4	5
Total	185	100	73	100

In the physician group, a favorable outcome was noted for 19 (95%) of the drug-dependent physicians, 16 (84%) of the physicians with alcoholism, and nine (64%) of physicians with a combined dependence (Table 2). These percentages were significantly different from the respective categories of the general group ($P<.05$, x^2). Although we are not clear why the physician group with combined dependence did less well, the degree of psychiatric disturbance may have had some effect. A previous study of 43 physicians noted evidence of a greater degree of psychopathology, as measured by the Minnesota Multiphasic Personality Inventory in the group dependent on both alcohol and other drugs.[15] We are unable to answer the important question, however, whether this evidence of psychopathology indicates preexisting psychiatric disturbance or reflects the mood and behavioral consequences of addiction to a number of drugs.

Of the 47 drug-abusing physicians, 19 (49%) used a single prescription drug, while 18 (38%) admitted to the use of three or more prescription drugs. The most commonly abused drugs were diazepam, 18 (38%), pentazocine, 15 (32%), and meperidine, 14 (30%). There was no distinct trend in the drug combinations used, as many physicians seemed to combine rather indiscriminately analgesics, tranquilizers, sedatives, and stimulants. When compared with 38 general patients who were drug-dependent, the physicians were more likely to use narcotics and less likely to use illegal street drugs.

Table 2.

Outcome Among 53 Physicians Treated for Alcoholism and Drug Dependence

Outcome	Alcohol Use Only		Drug Use Only		Both	
	No.	%	No.	%	No.	%
Abstinent	9	47	17	85	5	36
Brief relapse	7	37	2	10	4	29
Using but improving	2	11	1	5	2	14
Unimproved	1	5	0	0	3	21
Total	19	100	20	100	14	100

Table 3.

Types of Medical Practice of Physicians Treated for Alcoholism
and Drug Dependence

| | Physicians | | |
Type	No.	%	Percentage of Total US Physicians*
Family or general practice	24	33	14
Internal medicine	10	14	14
Psychiatry	6	8	7
Obstetric-gynecology	6	8	6
Anesthesiology	5	7	4
Surgery (general)	5	7	7
Radiology	4	5	5
Others	13	18	
Total	73	100	57

*Daily News *report, Oct 1, 1980, page 8.*

The proportion of the treated physicians in various types of medical practice as compared with the proportion of physicians in that practice for the country as a whole is given in Table 3. It is difficult to know how to interpret the distribution. The categorization and definition of "general practice" as a medical specialty continue to change; however, this group is overrepresented among our patients. The data may reflect the selection of physicians referred to our treatment program rather than indicate any definite trend of specialty vulnerability to addiction.

The physician group was further analyzed to determine whether the severity of alcohol or drug problem might predict outcome. When the outcomes of the 16 physicians who had mild problems (first admission for treatment, no obvious professional consequences) were compared with the outcomes of the 37 physicians who had more severe problems (multiple treatment admissions, obvious adverse professional consequences, such as loss of hospital privileges or licensure), there was no significant difference. Thirteen (81%) of the group with mild problems and 31 (84%) of the group with severe problems fared well. Therefore, the prognosis for addicted physicians probably is not related to the stage or severity of the disease.

Each Alcoholism and Drug Dependence patient was introduced to AA meetings and principles during treatment and was encouraged to become a member on dismissal. Although only 16 (31%) of the physician group became regular attenders, 100% of these had favorable outcomes. Twenty-nine (78%) of those who attended irregularly or did not attend at all were also in the favorable-outcome category.

Of the 53 physicians with adequate follow-up data, 47 (89%) had returned to the practice of medicine at the time of contact. Twenty (38%) had changed their practice in some way, often to a more structured setting, such as hospital-based or group practice. We are unable, however, to comment on the adequacy of their medical practice or the competence of the physician.

Comment

Our findings add to the growing documentation of favorable prognosis for the physician undergoing treatment of an addictive disorder (alcoholism and drug dependence). When compared with middle-class general patients undergoing similar treatment in the same program, physicians fared significantly better. We realize, however, that it is difficult to assess adequately treatment and prognosis of the addictions and agree with Westermeyer[16] in his conjecture that perhaps no area of medical care has been so poorly evaluated.

Our study has some limitations. The comparison groups were not treated concurrently, although there was overlap and the treatment program did not change overtly during the time in question. The physician group was contacted during a five-year period, and the general group was contacted one year after treatment. However, the mode of contact and follow-up was identical with each group. Furthermore, we relied mostly on self-report data, which were confirmed when possible by a relative, friend, or professional person. We continue to be skeptical of self-reports despite studies seeking to reassure. Polich,[17] for example, interpreting the well-analyzed Rand data, stated that his subjects accurately reported abstention and major alcohol-related events and concluded that these findings indicate the validity of most types of self-reports. This is notwithstanding his findings that 35% of recent drinkers underreported their consumption during the 24 hours before the interview and 24% underreported their consumption during the previous month.[17] Our clinical experience suggests a definite factor of unreliability in self-reports. However, we see no reason to suspect a greater error in one of our study groups than the other, therefore allowing relative comparisons.

We focused almost entirely on the abstinence or lack of abstinence from addicting drugs in our follow-up, realizing that this did not take into account such other important outcome measures as work adjustment, health status, interpersonal relationships, and social stability. However, other researchers have demonstrated a consistent correlation between these items and abstinence.[18]

Finally, the comparison groups were highly selected for positive outcome. Those who did not complete the inpatient phase of treatment were excluded, as were those who could not be contacted or were dead. However, few of the patients could not be reached (four [5%] of the physicians and three [2%] of the general group), and the death rates in the two groups seemed to be similar. We believe that it was reasonable to focus our attention on those patients motivated enough to complete inpatient treatment. It should be emphasized that reluctance to enter treatment seems almost universal because virtually all patients in both groups entered treatment under various forms of personal, social, medical, legal, or economic pressures. Few entered the hospital because of their own personal concern over the problem.

We believe it is important to note the lack of correlation between severity of addiction (as measured by adverse professional consequences and times previously treated) and treatment outcome. Physicians with multiple previous admissions and with severe professional difficulties recovered as favorably as did those with lesser problems. We believe this information should be made better known because it counteracts the reluctance of many to encourage treatment for addicts who have previously failed. It also provides some reassurance to state boards and impaired-physician committees that even the most severely addicted physician should receive an opportunity for adequate treatment.

Unexpected, and counteracting common opinion, was the highly favorable outcome of the drug-addicted physician. That the drug addict seemed to do better than the alcoholic patient is consistent with the results of Herrington et al,[12] who found that fewer narcotic-addicted physicians than alcoholic physicians experienced a significant or a brief relapse. Our data differ with those of the Menninger study,[10] which found no relationship between drugs of choice and treatment outcome. The group with the poorest outcome was the group with a combination of alcohol and drug dependence—a group that also seemed to have more evidence of psychopathology. However, the numbers in our study were small, and the difference may be a chance one.

What factors or influences might explain the reasons why physicians seem to recover from drug and alcohol addiction at higher rates than nonphysicians? Although we are unable to answer this with any of our data, we believe that basic intelligence, formal education, and type of occupation are not factors.

However, most of our physician patients, in contrast to the nonphysicians, were forced to begin their outpatient rehabilitation under a probationary reporting system. This may range from formal monitoring by the state licensure board, to review by hospital staff, to being overseen by concerned partners. Physicians are frequently asked to document aftercare visits and submit to random drug screens. Furthermore, many physicians are now also involved in the "impaired-physician" system, which brings them together in a group of similar professionals with similar problems. We believe that the structured monitoring system for the physician is therapeutic in itself and may enforce longer periods of abstinence from drugs and alcohol, during which time other rehabilitation efforts can become effective and the behavioral effects of addiction can moderate.

Similar systems are available to nonphysicians only under special circumstances. The Federal Aviation Administration and the airline companies place strong sanctions on airline pilots, prohibiting flying status while under the influence of alcohol or other drugs. Pilots treated for chemical dependency are monitored closely during the recovery period, under methods similar to those used with physicians. The director of The Employee Assistance Program for a national airline has noted a recovery rate of 90% among more than 100 treated pilots followed in a preliminary survey. Of theoretical interest is the shared threat of loss of highly valued professional privileges in the two groups—flying status for the pilot and practice privilege for the physician. Perhaps the motivation to recover is stronger when the occupation at risk is high status, competitively sought, and identified closely with personal image and prestige.

References

1. AMA Council on Mental Health: The sick physician: Impairment of psychiatric disorders, including alcoholism and drug dependence. *JAMA* 1973;223:684–687.

2. Duffy JC, Litin EM: Psychiatric morbidity of physicians. *JAMA* 1964;189:989–992.

3. Hurt RD, Morse RM, Swenson WM: Diagnosis of alcoholism with a self-administered alcoholism screening test: Results with 1,002 consecutive patients receiving general examinations. *Mayo Clin Proc* 1980;55:365–370.

4. Niven RG, Hurt RD, Morse RM, et al: Alcoholism in physicians. *Mayo Clin Proc* 1984;59:12–16.

5. De Luca JR (ed): *Alcohol and Health*. Rockville, Md, Dept of Health and Human Services, 1981.

6. Vaillant GE, Brighton JR, McArthur C: Physicians' use of mood-altering drugs: A 20-year follow-up report. *N Engl J Med* 1970;282:365–370.

7. Swanson DW, Weddige RI, Morse RM: Hospitalized pentazocine abusers. *Mayo Clin Proc* 1973;48:85–93.

8. Swanson DW, Weddige RI, Morse RM: Abuse of prescription drugs. *Mayo Clin Proc* 1973;48:359–367.

9. Goby MJ, Bradley NJ, Bespalec DA: Physicians treated for alcoholism: A follow-up study. *Alcoholism* 1979;3:121–124.

10. Johnson RP, Connelly JC: Addicted Physicians: A closer look. *JAMA* 1981;245:253–257.

11. Kliner DJ, Spicer J, Barnett P: Treatment outcome of alcoholic physicians. *J Stud Alcohol* 1980;41:1217–1219.

12. Herrington RE, Benzer DG, Jacobson GR, et al: Treating substance-use disorders among physicians. *JAMA* 1982;247:2253–2257.

13. Dietvorst TF, Swenson WM, Morse RM: Intellectual assessment in a midwestern alcoholism treatment population. *J Clin Psychol* 1978;34:244–249.

14. Pendery ML, Maltzman IM, West LJ: Controlled drinking by alcoholics? New findings and a reevaluation of a major affirmative study. *Science* 1982;217:169–175.

15. Dietvorst TF, Swenson WM, Niven RG et al: Analysis of the MMPI profiles of physicians in treatment for drug dependency. *J Stud Alcohol* 1979;40:1023–1029.

16. Westermeyer J: *A Primer on Chemical Dependency: A Clinical*

Guide to Alcohol and Drug Problems. Baltimore, Williams & Wilkins Co, 1976.

17. Polich JM: The validity of self-reports in alcoholism research. *Addict Behav* 1982;7:123–132.

18. Baekeland F: Evaluation of treatment methods in chronic alcoholism, in Kissin B, Begleiter H (eds): *The Biology of Alcoholism,* New York, Plenum Press, 1977, Vol 5, pp 385–440.

The Definition of Alcoholism

ROBERT M. MORSE, MD; DANIEL K. FLAVIN, MD; FOR
THE JOINT COMMITTEE OF THE NATIONAL COUNCIL ON
ALCOHOLISM AND DRUG DEPENDENCE AND THE AMERICAN
SOCIETY OF ADDICTION MEDICINE TO STUDY THE DEFINITION
AND CRITERIA FOR THE DIAGNOSIS OF ALCOHOLISM

To establish a more precise use of the term alcoholism, *a 23-member multidisciplinary committee of the National Council on Alcoholism and Drug Dependence and the American Society of Addiction Medicine conducted a 2-year study of the definition of alcoholism in the light of current concepts. The goals of the committee were to create by consensus a revised definition that is (1) scientifically valid, (2) clinically useful, and (3) understandable by the general public. Therefore, the committee agreed to define alcoholism as a primary, chronic disease with genetic, psychosocial, and environmental factors influencing its development and manifestations. The disease is often progressive and fatal. It is characterized by impaired control over drinking, preoccupation with the drug alcohol, use of alcohol despite adverse consequences, and distortions in thinking, most notably denial. Each of these symptoms may be continuous or periodic.*

(*JAMA.* 1992;268:1012–1014)

In 1972, the National Council on Alcoholism (NCA, now called the National Council on Alcoholism and Drug Dependence) published its seminal article entitled "Criteria for the Diagnosis of Alcoholism."[1] This was followed in 1976 by the "Definition of Alcoholism,"[2] prepared by the Committee on Definitions of the National Council on Alcoholism and the American Medical Society on Alcoholism (now called the American Society of Addiction Medicine). This definition emphasized the progressive nature of alcoholism, the physical sequelae

Originally published in Journal of the American Medical Association (JAMA) *268, no. 8 (26 August 1992): 1012–1014. Copyrighted 1992, American Medical Association. Reprinted with permission.*

of alcohol use, and the phenomena of tolerance and withdrawal: "Alcoholism is a chronic, progressive, and potentially fatal disease. It is characterized by tolerance and physical dependency or pathologic organ changes, or both—all the direct or indirect consequences of the alcohol ingested." The authors of this definition also clarified and defined several concepts, including use of the terms *chronic and progressive, tolerance, physical dependency,* and *pathologic organ changes.*

Our knowledge in this area has not remained static, however, and many strides have been made toward understanding alcoholism since the creation of the National Institute on Alcohol Abuse and Alcoholism in 1970. Some of us have even become impatient for definitive answers to questions about the causes of and cures for alcoholism. Therefore, we must be reminded by Gordis[3] of the "discovery curve." From basic research to clinical practice, the natural course of scientific discovery is a progressive and time-consuming process. One insight gradually leads to another so that, with thoughtful direction and steady support, progress continues. Thus, important contributions, such as the strong evidence for neurogenetic mechanisms in alcoholism[4,5] or the modulation of alcohol intake by neurotransmitter (serotonin) inhibitors [6,7] have yet to pay off in terms of clinical usefulness. In addition to research advances, continuing efforts to develop a uniform, reliable classification system have led to a modification of terms and to clarification of concepts used to describe alcohol-related problems and alcoholism.[8] In this context, the 1976 definition emphasized the physiologic sequelae of alcohol use and failed to recognize the spectrum of biopsychosocial factors that influence the development of alcoholism and its manifestations.

The *Diagnostic and Statistical Manual of Mental Disorders, Third Edition, Revised*[9] *(DSM-III-R)* of the American Psychiatric Association and the *International Classification of Diseases Ninth Revision (ICD-9)*[10] of the World Health Organization have emphasized the concept of "alcohol dependence," introduced in 1976 by Edwards and Gross[11] as "alcohol dependence syndrome," rather than the term *alcoholism.* At the time, Edwards and Gross[11] noted that the diagnostic use of the term *alcoholism,* as then defined, was overinclusive and dependent on the mercurial, value-laden concept of disease. Alcohol dependence syndrome is based on the more specific formulation that an occurrence of a clinical phenomenon distinct from (but not mutually exclusive of) alcohol related disabilities (and consequences or both) is recognizable and quantifiable. The alcohol dependence syndrome, as described by Edwards and Gross, is characterized by narrowing of the drinking repertoire, salience of drink-seeking behavior, increased tolerance, repeated withdrawal symptoms, relief and avoidance of withdrawal symptoms, subjective awareness of a compulsion to drink, and reinstatement (of drinking) after abstinence. Both the *DSM-III-R*[9] and the proposed 10th revision of the *International Classification of Diseases*[12] include, in addition to alcohol dependence syndrome, criteria referring to persistent drinking despite adverse consequences (or "problems," as in *DSM-III-R).*

Despite this diagnostic use of the term *alcohol dependence,* the term *alcoholism* continues to be widely used among professionals and the general public alike. Alcoholism is vaguely referred to under "patterns of use" in *DSM-III-R.* Yet it is not directly compared or contrasted with the terms *alcohol dependency* and *alcohol abuse.* Thus, it remains unclear whether these concepts are interchangeable or inconsistent with each other.

To establish a more precise use of the term *alcoholism,* the National Council on Alcoholism and Drug Dependence and the American Society of Addiction Medicine created a Joint Committee to Study the Definition and Criteria for the Diagnosis of Alcoholism. This 23-member multidisciplinary group (scientists, physicians, and lay leaders) formulated a revised definition of alcoholism that the group hoped would be (1) scientifically valid, (2) clinically useful, and (3) understandable by the general public. Clearly, this is a difficult task and one that is necessarily ongoing and incomplete. Well-intentioned scientists continue to debate basic concepts of alcoholism. Some argue that it is mainly a disorder of appetite, that is, a pathologic or abnormal appetite (not present in non-alcoholics) for a particular substance.[3] Others, after the work of Wikler,[13] emphasize the principles of classical conditioning. Physicians from the various specialties, such as psychiatry and internal medicine, tend to view alcoholism from slightly different perspectives, and some of the informed lay public disagree with the above concepts and focus instead on the cultural, legal, or moral aspects of alcoholism. That the joint committee could arrive at a consensus is a tribute to the persistence, open-mindedness, and goodwill of its members. Without undertaking an exhaustive scientific review of the subject, we at least hoped not to be at odds with currently known and accepted concepts in this rapidly evolving field.

The revised definition proposed by the committee recognizes alcoholism as a heterogeneous disease (that is, biopsychosocial factors are implicated in the causes, signs and symptoms, complications, and treatment of alcoholism). The definition acknowledges a genetic vulnerability in the evolution of alcoholism in many alcoholics; broadens the scope of the 1976 definition to include the basic behavioral changes that are symptomatic of the disease; and, for the first time, formally incorporates denial as a major concept. By giving greater consideration to these factors, the committee hopes that the revised definition will encourage earlier intervention in the course of alcoholism by professionals and the general population. The revised definition of alcoholism more closely approximates that of alcohol dependence as outlined in *DSM-III-R*[9] and the proposed 10th revision of the *International Classification of Diseases.*[12] Although the term *alcoholism* has been used over the years as a vague, poorly understood, and sometimes morally flavored term, we do not believe it necessary or desirable to discard it. Rather, we prefer to clarify its meaning with updated concepts and terminology so that its usage will be more meaningful.

Revised Definition of Alcoholism

Alcoholism is a primary, chronic disease with genetic, psychosocial, and environmental factors influencing its development and manifestations. The disease is often progressive and fatal. It is characterized by impaired control over drinking, preoccupation with the drug alcohol, use of alcohol despite adverse consequences, and distortions in thinking, most notably denial. Each of these symptoms may be continuous or periodic.

"Primary" refers to the nature of alcoholism as a disease entity in addition to and separate from other pathophysiologic states that may be associated with it. It suggests that as an addiction, alcoholism is not a symptom of an underlying disease state.

"Disease" means an involuntary disability. Use of the term *involuntary* in defining disease is descriptive of this state as a discrete entity that is not deliberately pursued. It does not suggest passivity in the recovery process. Similarly, use of this term does not imply the abrogation of responsibility in the legal sense. Disease represents the sum of the abnormal phenomenon displayed by the group of individuals. These phenomena are associated with a specified common set of characteristics by which certain individuals differ from the norm and which places them at a disadvantage.[14]

"Often progressive and fatal" means that the disease persists over time and that physical, emotional, and social changes are often cumulative and may progress as drinking continues. Alcoholism causes premature death through overdose; through organic complications involving the brain, liver, heart, and other organs; and by contributing to suicide, homicide, motor vehicle accidents, and other traumatic events.

"Impaired control" means the inability to consistently limit on drinking occasions the duration of the drinking episode, the quantity of alcohol consumed, and/or the behavioral consequences.

"Preoccupation" used in association with "alcohol use" indicates excessive, focused attention given to the drug alcohol and to its effects or its use (or both). The relative value the person assigns to alcohol often leads to energy being diverted from important life concerns.

"Adverse consequences" are alcohol-related problems, "disabilities," or impairments in such areas as physical health (eg, alcohol withdrawal syndromes, liver disease, gastritis, anemia, and neurologic disorders), psychologic functioning (eg, cognition and changes in mood and behavior), interpersonal functioning (eg, marital problems, child abuse, and troubled social relationships), occupational functioning (eg, scholastic or job problems), and legal, financial, or spiritual problems. Although the alcohol dependence syndrome may theoretically occur in the absence of adverse consequences, we believe that the latter are evident in virtually all clinical cases.

"Denial" is used in the definition not only in the psychoanalytic sense of a single psychologic defense mechanism disavowing the significance of events but more broadly to include a range of psychologic maneuvers that decrease awareness of the fact that alcohol use is the cause of a person's problems rather than a solution to those problems. Denial becomes an integral part of the disease and is nearly always a major obstacle to recovery. Denial in alcoholism is a complex phenomenon determined by multiple psychologic and physiologic mechanisms. These include the pharmacologic effects of alcohol on memory, the influence of euphoric recall on perception and insight, the role of suppression and repression as psychologic defense mechanisms, and the impact of social and cultural enabling behavior.

Our proposed definition should not be interpreted as a new

set of criteria for making the diagnosis of alcoholism, even though certain criteria are implied in its terminology.

Comment

In 1972, the "Criteria for the Diagnosis of Alcoholism" (authored by the Criteria Committee of the NCA) appeared in simultaneous publications in the *American Journal of Psychiatry* and the *Annals of Internal Medicine*.[1,15] This document summarized the ideas then current and set the stage for thinking about alcoholism by making pertinent reference to several matters that previously had been avoided or left obscure. These included the simple but encompassing concept of alcoholism as a pathologic dependency on alcohol; a review of the nature of alcoholism as a disease; the recommendation that a separate psychiatric diagnosis should be made for every patient, apart from the diagnosis of alcoholism; the assertion that because alcoholism is chronic and relapsing, no reference should be made to a "complete cure" but rather the outcome may be categorized as recovered, arrested, or in remission; and a warning that alcoholics are at high risk for cross dependence (or cross addiction) on other drugs.

For the first time, the diagnosis of alcoholism was said to be obligatory when certain conditions were met. For example, diagnostic level 1 included withdrawal seizures, delirium tremens, or alcoholic hepatitis. Alcoholism was also an obligatory diagnosis when drinking continued despite strong, identified social contraindications, such as marriage disruption. However, the criteria proved troublesome in several areas. Dividing diagnostic criteria into physiologic-clinical (track 1) and behavioral-psychologic and attitudinal (track 2) was clear, but subdividing these into major and minor categories became obscure. Furthermore, the diagnostic levels (1, 2, and 3) were vague and overlapped as they progressed from "obligatory" to "probable" to "possible." Subdividing the criteria further into direct or indirect effects of alcohol raised other questions. An attempt to categorize early and late stages also became problematic when, for example, defense mechanisms such as denial were classified as late-stage alcoholism.

The original NCA criteria mainly focused on the adverse consequences of drinking as the basic criteria for alcoholism. These criteria did not take into consideration the concept of an alcohol dependence syndrome that may be present apart from the consequences ("disabilities") of drinking. Although the NCA criteria clearly represented an important benchmark in developing efforts to clarify concepts of alcoholism, they are deficient by current standards. Efforts to improve and modify the extensive diagnostic criteria of *DSM-III-R*[9] and *ICD-9*[10] are progressing through the respective parent organizations. We encourage and will attempt to influence these persistent, scholarly, and scientific endeavors.

In regard to these recent formulations of the alcohol dependence syndrome *(DSM-III-R and ICD-9)*, we are concerned about and draw attention to the following issues:

1. Although *alcoholism* is occasionally referred to by name, no attempt is made to clarify whether this is synonymous with *alcohol dependence* or *alcohol abuse* nor is there any discussion about how these terms are interrelated. In the *Diagnostic and Statistical Manual of Mental Disorders, Third Edition,*[16] *alcohol dependence* was equated with *alcoholism*.
2. The terminology remains awkward. *Psychoactive substance dependence,* for example, might easily be called *addictive disorder* or *drug dependence*.
3. *Abuse* is a term objectionable to many. An alternative suggestion is "alcohol use with [description of effect]," for example, "alcohol use with intoxication," as suggested by the 1972 NCA criteria. Or, as noted by Kleber,[17] several terms could be substituted, including *unsanctioned use, hazardous use, dysfunctional use,* and *harmful use*.

4. *DSM-III-R*[9] comprehensively describes dependence as a "cluster of cognitive, behavioral, and physiologic symptoms that indicate . . . impaired control of (alcohol) and continued use . . . despite adverse consequences." However, it then allows the diagnosis of alcohol dependence to be made by any three of nine distinct criteria. This variability seems to imply the lack of a core or central concept for the disorder. Grant[18] has calculated that 466 unique subtypes are possible when the diagnosis is allowed by any three or more of the criteria.

5. Denial and other psychologic defense mechanisms are not mentioned, even though they are a consistent clinical component of the alcoholic syndrome.

6. If tolerance is to be emphasized and even quantified, as in *DSM-III-R*,[9] then changed tolerance (ie, a decreased tolerance in the elderly or chronic alcoholic or a dramatic increase) should also be mentioned in the criteria.

7. Medical and physiologic disorders should receive more prominence. Alcoholic liver disease and delirium tremens are pathognomonic of alcoholism and should be interpreted as such.

8. Although it is not implied that alcoholism is a symptom of another disorder, we believe it is important that the diagnostic criteria, particularly in psychiatry, formally recognize alcoholism, a prototype addiction, to be a primary disorder. This might naturally lead to a clarification of the disease concept of alcoholism, which is an important consideration in the development of diagnostic criteria.[19–21]

The definition of alcoholism was prepared by Robert M. Morse, MD, Daniel K. Flavin, MD, and the Joint Committee of the National Council on Alcoholism and Drug Dependence and the American Society of Addiction Medicine to Study the Definition and Criteria for the Diagnosis of Alcoholism. The committee comprised Daniel J. Anderson, PhD; Margaret

Bean-Bayog, MD; Henri Begleiter, MD, PhD; Sheila B. Blume, MD, CAC; Jean Forest, MD; Stanley E. Gitlow, MD; Enoch Gordis, MD; James E. Kelsey, MD; Nancy K. Mello, PhD; Roger E. Meyer, MD; Robert G. Niven, MD; Ann Noll; Barton Pakul, MD; Katherine K. Pike; Lucy Barry Robe; Max A. Schneider, MD; Marc Schuckit, MD; David E. Smith, MD; Emanuel M. Steindler; Boris Tabakoff, PhD; and George Vaillant, MD; James Callahan, DPA; Jasper Chen-See, MD; and Robert D. Sparks, MD, members ex officio; and Frank A. Seixas, MD, emeritus consultant.

References

1. Criteria Committee, National Council on Alcoholism. "Criteria for the diagnosis of alcoholism." *Ann Intern Med.* 1972;77:249–258.
2. National Council on Alcoholism/American Medical Society on Alcoholism Committee on Definitions. "Definition of alcoholism." *Ann Intern Med.* 1976;85:764.
3. Gordis E. "Alcoholism and scientific progress." *Alcohol Health Res World.* 1989;13:298–300.
4. Cloniger CR. "Neurogenetic adaptive mechanisms in alcoholism." *Science.* 1987;236:410–416.
5. Cloniger CR, Bohman M, Sigvardsson S. "Inheritance of alcohol abuse: cross-fostering analysis of adopted men." *Arch Gen Psychiatry.* 1981;38:861–868.
6. Naranjo CA, Sellers EM, Lawrin MO. "Modulation of ethanol intake by serotonin uptake inhibitors." *J Clin Psychiatry.* 1986;47(suppl):16–22.
7. Le AD, Khanna JM, Kalant H, LeBlanc, AE. "Effect of modification of brain serotonin (5–HT), norepinephrine (NE) and dopamine (DA) on ethanol tolerance." *Psychopharmacology (Berl).* 1981;75:231–235.
8. World Health Organization. "Nomenclature and classification of drug- and alcohol-related problems: a WHO memorandum." *Bull World Health Organ.* 1981;59:225–242.
9. American Psychiatric Association, Committee on Nomenclature

and Statistics. *Diagnostic and Statistical Manual of Mental Disorders, Third Edition, Revised.* Washington, DC: American Psychiatric Association, 1987.

10. World Health Organization. *Mental Disorders: Glossary and Guide to Their Classification in Accordance With the Ninth Revision of the International Classification of Diseases.* Geneva, Switzerland: World Health Organization, 1978.

11. Edwards G, Gross MM. "Alcohol dependence: provisional description of a clinical syndrome." *BMJ.* 1976;1:1058–1061.

12. National Institute on Alcohol Abuse and Alcoholism. *Seventh Special Report to the US Congress on Alcohol and Health.* Rockville, Md: US Dept of Health and Human Services, 1990.

13. Wikler A. "Dynamics of drug dependence: implications of a conditioning theory for research and treatment." *Arch Gen Psychiatry.* 1973;28:611–616.

14. Campbell EJM, Scadding JG, Roberts RS. "The concept of disease." *BMJ.* 1979;2:757–762.

15. Criteria Committee, National Council on Alcoholism. "Criteria for the diagnosis of alcoholism." *Am J Psychiatry.* 1972;129:127–135.

16. American Psychiatric Association, Committee on Nomenclature and Statistics. *Diagnostic and Statistical Manual of Mental Disorders, Third Edition.* Washington, DC: American Psychiatric Association, 1980.

17. Kleber HD. "The nosology of abuse and dependence." *J Psychiatr Res.* 1990;24(suppl 2):57–64.

18. Grant BF. "DSM-III-R and ICD-10 classification of alcohol use disorders and associated disabilities: a structural analysis." *Int Rev Psychiatr.* 1989;1:21–39.

19. Jellinek EM. *The Disease Concept of Alcoholism.* New Haven, Conn: Hillhouse Press, 1960:33–41.

20. Morse RM. "The disease concept controversy: is there a cure?" *Subst Abuse.* 1989;10:75–76.

21. Meyer RE. "Overview of the concept of alcoholism." In: Rose RM, Barrett JE, eds. *Alcoholism: Origins and Outcome.* New York, NY: Raven Press, 1988:1–14.

Courtesy Hazelden-Pittman Archives

Alcoholism—A Spiritual Illness

As a theology student, Gordon Grimm questioned his pastoral calling in life. But once he had a chance to get involved in clinical work with recovering alcoholics, he found a challenge that matched his own search for spirituality. During his three decades at Hazelden, Grimm became one of the principal creators and supporters of the pastoral and spiritual dimension in the Minnesota Model of treatment, and he designed a clinical pastoral education program that was renowned as the preeminent training center for clergy who worked with chemical dependents.

Early Years

Gordon (Gordy) Grimm was born in Sac City, Iowa, on July 1, 1933. His parents, Beulah Eleanor Wilson and Homer Eugene Grimm, had two other children, who were younger than Gordy. Jay was born in 1934, and Julie was born in 1940. Grimm's father graduated from Iowa State University with a degree in electrical engineering. As a student, Homer first met Beulah at a football game at the University of Iowa. They married on Flag Day, June 28, 1928. When Homer finished college, the young couple moved to Kenosha, Wisconsin, where Homer got a job as an electrician. After the stockmarket collapsed in 1929 they moved to Sac City to live on the farm of Grandpa Wilson, Beulah's father. When the depression

---

Child's Play

Grimm fondly remembers the creek that ran through their land, where he and his brother mischievously filled their pockets with the small green snakes that infested the water. The boys would give the snakes to the hogs, which ran amuck feeding on them. One time their clothes were so dirty and wet from romping around the creek catching snakes that their mother collared them before they could empty their pockets. She had them take off their clothes and put them in the washing machine. Later, when Beulah found the snakes floating on top of the water, she gave both her sons a sound thrashing with a broom handle.

---

forced them to give up that farm in 1937, the family moved to the homestead of their other grandparents, in Clear Lake, Iowa, and settled in a home next door to Grandma Grimm.

These years on the farm kindled in Grimm a great love for the land. For a time he wanted to be a farmer, following in the footsteps of his two grandfathers. When he wasn't in school, Grimm was doing chores on the farm, work that he thoroughly enjoyed. He was an officer in 4–H and became a livestock judge. In 1950 he was the only high school student who placed in the top twenty-five contestants for judging combined livestock. In 1951 he went to the American Royal Livestock Exposition as a judge representing Ventura High School.

Grimm's parents influenced his religious development in a number of ways, all of which had a bearing on his later beliefs and practices. His father was Lutheran, and his mother was Methodist, the religion in which he was baptized. Eventually, the Lutheran church that Grimm's father attended removed him from the membership roster because of his alcoholism. This made Grimm so angry at all institutional churches that, as a sophomore in high school, he ceased being an active member of the Methodist church. On the one hand, Grimm felt deeply hurt and disappointed by his father's unpredictable behavior. On the other hand, he already had a sense at this early age—long before he started working with alcoholics—

that alcoholism was not something that was morally reprehensible. He felt that churches should take a more compassionate and forgiving stance toward the alcoholic, in this case his father.

In contrast to his compassionate feelings for his father, Grimm harbored a lot of anger toward his mother, especially during his adolescence and young adulthood. By 1951 circumstances at home had become so tense due to alcoholism that Grimm's father left. Although Grimm did not fully understand the intensity of his emotions, he blamed the departure of his father on his mother. Later, he realized that it was his mother who had worked hard and sacrificed to keep the family together, and he came to see her life as an example of the courage and patience that he needed as he pursued his own ministry of helping others.

College

Although he had an initial inclination to go to Purdue University, Grimm decided to register at Morningside College, a Methodist institution in Sioux City, Iowa, in order to pursue courses in animal husbandry. But he decided after only a few days there in the fall of 1951 that this school choice was not to his liking, especially when he discovered that two of his mother's relatives were on the board of trustees. On his way home he passed his father's alma mater, Iowa State, and considered going there. Despite the grief his father had caused him, Grimm harbored a great affection for his dad. Nevertheless, Grimm decided against Iowa State, feeling that it was too big and too impersonal.

After returning home, Grimm escorted his friend and high school classmate Lyle Hall to Luther College in Decorah, Iowa, to help him settle in. While having lunch in the school cafeteria, Grimm met the football coach, Esel Zweizer. The coach, impressed with Grimm's size, offered him a chance to play football at Luther (though the college did not offer any athletic scholarships). Zweizer was a great coach who was able to inspire young men to play simply for the love of the game, and Grimm decided to accept his offer. The following year he enrolled as a physics major, but, after a year of struggling with calculus, he changed to economics and shortly after that to ancient history. In his first two years he dressed for football and started three games. But a shoulder injury and broken ribs prompted him to drop varsity sports and concentrate on intramurals, where he discovered he had just as much fun.

At Luther Grimm became friends with a preseminary student named Harley Swiggum, who was ten years older than Grimm. Swiggum's life and religious conversion had a strong influence on Grimm, who otherwise was not impressed with most of the preseminarians at Luther. Swiggum lived in Milwaukee, where Grimm's father also lived and worked as a railroad electrician. Occasionally Grimm would accompany Swiggum on trips to Milwaukee in order to visit his father. While only an occasional churchgoer, his father, nevertheless, was a devout and daily reader of the Bible on his own search for God. He believed that the Scriptures contained all one needed to know about God, while, despite claims to the contrary, no church contained all the truth about God. Grimm remembers being curious about the many personal annotations that his father had written in the Bible that rested on his bed stand.

In 1957, his father paid a rare visit to the family while Grimm was home for Thanksgiving. While there he underwent a physical examination, a prerequisite for a job promotion for which he had been recommended. The clean bill of health that he received was no warranty against his dying of a heart attack three days later.

Luther College had an active Lutheran Student Association, a youth religious organization involved in social-service activities. Although Grimm rarely participated in the group during his first two years at Luther, on one of the rare occasions when he did, he met Christine Rolto, the sister of his roommate, Ted. She asked him if he would be willing to teach Sunday school at a mission church in Burchnall, which was close to his home, during his second summer vacation. He agreed and was deeply impressed by the experience. The people were poor but possessed a strong and active faith. Grimm discovered that the children really knew their Bible. This experience helped motivate him to think about entering the seminary.

Other people also influenced his thoughts about seminary. Besides Swiggum, two other college friends, Jim Burquist and Myland Davis, chose the seminary at the same time. Grimm's girlfriend,

Darlene, persuaded him to go to church with her occasionally. At her urging he took instructions and subsequently was confirmed in the Lutheran Church. His friends were motivated by the desire to make the world a better place, and that impressed Grimm. He saw them as good human beings who wanted to enjoy life and at the same time serve God. In the spring semester of his third year of college, Grimm decided to go on to the seminary. When he told his mother, she was moved to tears, partially out of joy because of her deep faith and partially out of fear. As she told her son, "You will have to deal with money, and you will never be able to satisfy people." Somewhat prophetically, Grimm told her that he would probably never have a parish.

Seminary

Grimm began his first year at Luther Theological Seminary in St. Paul, Minnesota, in August 1956. As a freshman he received the honor of being selected to participate in an ecumenical dialogue with the Benedictines at St. John's University in Collegeville, Minnesota. While the exchanges were the highlight of the year for him, he also entertained serious doubts about becoming a pastor. Twice he sought to leave but was persuaded to give it some more time.

When Grimm thought about leaving the third time, he met with Alvin Rogness, the president of the seminary. Rogness had a great reputation both for his ecumenical efforts with Catholics on behalf of the working class in Mason City, Iowa, and for his casual manner of dressing in old and unpressed clothes. He told Grimm that if he were really going to leave, then this time he should burn his bridges and be done with this indecisiveness. As a last resort, Rogness sent him to see Fritz Norsted, who was in charge of pastoral programs and head of the chaplains at Lutheran Social Services. Norsted prevailed upon Grimm to get a taste of pastoral work before he made a final decision.

Norsted placed Grimm in a clinical pastoral education program, in which he would learn about the work of chaplains in hospital settings. This placement was very unusual for a first-year theology student, but it allowed Grimm the opportunity to sort out some of the personal issues he felt about his mother and father. He also had his first insights into how important it was for a clergy person to have a strong and growing knowledge of himself and his inner spirit to prepare him for helping others. This taste enabled Grimm to make a commitment to the clergy and to clinical pastoral education. He spent the following summer at Fergus Falls Hospital, furthering his clinical pastoral education under the supervision of Herb Skari.

Grimm's third year internship, in the summer of 1958, was spent first at Samaritan Hospital in St. Paul and then at Willmar State Hospital in rural Minnesota, where Nelson Bradley and Dan Anderson were introducing a new, multidisciplinary program for the treatment of alcoholics. Grimm's pastoral ministry was supervised by the Reverend John Keller, a close colleague of Bradley and Anderson and a participant in the multidisciplinary approach to treatment. At Willmar, Grimm roomed with Dick Heilman, M.D., who later consulted at Hazelden and supervised the Chemical Dependency Center at the Veteran's Hospital in Minneapolis. Fred Eiden, a recovering counselor, was very helpful to Grimm, and he gave Grimm a big compliment when he told him that he was amazingly free of judgment even though he was a religious person. Grimm believed his ability to be nonjudgmental had its beginnings in his relationship with his father.

At the end of the summer, Grimm returned to the seminary, where he continued his academic studies in theology. The following summer, he accompanied Gene Rossi, a psychologist on the staff at Willmar, to the Yale Summer School of Alcohol Studies. To earn some money during his fourth and final year of seminary, Grimm worked as an assistant to the dean at Augsburg College. He finished his theological and pastoral studies in a class of 130 students.

Before ordination, the students were required to pass their colloquium, which was attended by all the Lutheran bishops in the United States. Each student had to appear individually before a committee of three bishops for an examination on Lutheran doctrine and the confession. Grimm was worried that he might be questioned on infant baptism, which he had a problem with because the practice could not be found in Scripture. He managed to set the bishops arguing the issue among themselves, thereby avoiding a formal reprimand or even a scolding. He was ordained in the

Lutheran Church on September 20, 1960. Before being called to the special work demanded by a chaplaincy, the newly ordained generally had to wait three years, during which they were expected to gain some general pastoral experience. But an exception was made in Grimm's case, and he was assigned to Willmar State Hospital, replacing John Keller, who had gone with Bradley to Lutheran General Hospital in Chicago.

Willmar State Hospital

Grimm's summer internship at Willmar had already introduced him to the multidisciplinary work of Nelson Bradley and Dan Anderson. This psychiatrist-psychologist team had been working to erase the notion of alcoholism as a psychiatric condition. Bradley separated the alcoholics from the mentally ill at Willmar, left their doors unlocked, and allowed AA members to talk with the patients. In 1954, Bradley and Anderson had convinced the Minnesota State Legislature to create paid positions for counselors on alcoholism, which would be held by nondegreed lay people—recovering alcoholics— who would share responsibility for a treatment program and have an equal say with the professional staff. At the time this was a radical change, to go from a physician-oriented, psychoanalytic hospital to a treatment program conducted by "drunks." Bradley and Anderson also recognized that the clergy had a certain stability and could easily be trained to help alcoholics with their self-inventories (Steps Four and Five).

When Grimm returned to Willmar in 1960, he was the only chaplain assigned to the alcoholic wards, which had 240 patients. His sense of isolation was compounded by the fact that he was not certain what his role and duties might be in dealing with alcoholics. What special religious needs did they have? Grimm struggled with his own understanding of alcoholism and the spiritual and pastoral needs of the alcoholic. It put him off stride to see that AA was so meaningful to these patients while religion was irrelevant. His comprehension of the meaning and spirituality of the Twelve Steps underwent a slow but steady maturation.

As Grimm sought to legitimize the relevance and need for pastoral care for the alcoholic he relied on three sources: (1) his own common sense to adapt his theological training to the needs of alcoholics, (2) other clergy working with alcoholics, and (3) the recovering counselors, especially Fred Eiden, who always had time for Grimm when he demonstrated that he really wanted to learn what alcoholism and recovery were all about.

On one occasion, Eiden and Grimm went on a retreat conducted by Fritz Norsted, Bill Currens, and John Keller for an audience that included mainly recovering alcoholics. Eiden talked quite freely about his background with Grimm and after the retreat indicated that Norsted had made a deep impression on him. He said that Norsted's presentation helped rid him of a great deal of his hostility toward God. Norsted, unlike most clergy, did not try to force God upon people when He was already there.

Most of the counselors at Willmar were covertly hostile toward religion and displayed a coolness toward pastors and chaplains. They regarded them as proselytizers seeking converts among the alcoholics for their denominational practices. For example, a counselor named Maxwell Lowell taught Grimm a great deal about AA spirituality, but whenever Grimm raised the subject of religion, Lowell would walk away. Grimm was heartened, however, when certain counselors at Willmar began to send their patients to the "spirituality" groups on prayer that he conducted. As Grimm immersed himself in the spirituality of AA, he began to realize that most of the recovering counselors did not realize, or ignored the fact, that the spiritual practices inherent in the Steps had long been part of the Judaic-Christian tradition of spirituality.

Grimm also learned much from a series of lectures introduced at Willmar by Bradley for the benefit of the staff and the community at large. One was on the Fourth and Fifth Steps, and another was on sponsorship. The counselors would share with Grimm their own personal experiences in taking those Steps. Eiden offered to role model for the theological students in the clinical pastoral education program what a Fifth Step should be like. Father Bernard Lenarze, an associate of Grimm's, stressed that the Fifth Step was not a religious rite even though it might resemble the sacrament of confession in the Catholic Church. At that time there was no written material for the clergy to work with, and Grimm had not yet discovered the importance of the Big Book, with its relevant pages on the Fifth Step.

Most clergy missed the point in those days regarding the work that could be done for alcoholics. It took the clergy awhile to recognize that alcoholism was a disease and not a moral issue. Like Grimm, other clergy dedicated to helping alcoholics were trying to find their way. Lenarze at first compared recovery to a religious practice during the Lenten season. The alcoholic was giving up drink in order to straighten out the rest of his or her life. John Keller, the Lutheran chaplain at Willmar before Grimm, believed that the AA slogan "Twenty-four hours a day" corresponded to the Scriptural belief that *daily* the old Adam must die. The Jesuit theologian John Ford believed that most alcoholics wanted an act of God to convert them, much like Saint Paul and Bill W had experienced. But Ford himself believed that recovery was a gradual, day-by-day process.

During these years, Grimm tossed back and forth between the spirituality of AA and the Christian religion. Did the two go together, or did people have to choose between one or the other? Or, as others had suggested to him, were these two fellowships, or kingdoms, that sometimes overlapped and sometimes did not? This latter counsel was helpful to him in distinguishing between the spiritual and the religious or denominational dimensions of a person's search for wholeness. Gradually Grimm adopted and internalized a pastoral approach based on two kingdoms or fellowships that sometimes overlapped and sometimes did not.

Finding His Pastoral Role

The Lutheran emphasis on the Word and the Sacrament and on the presence of Christ in the Eucharist was very important to Grimm. Relying on his religious tradition, he made a commitment to contact all of the Lutheran patients at Willmar and provide them individually with the Sacrament if they wished to receive it. At least ministering the Sacrament was a justification for his presence and his ministry at the hospital.

Still, he felt that something was lacking in his ministry, and he did not know what it was. The religious language used by the Church was not helpful, and the treatment language of "tough love" and "personal responsibility" became a part of his spiritual vocabulary only gradually. He felt that the alcoholics' needs were more in the line of counseling (which can be a way of preaching), but initially he was unable to adapt the Word to the needs of the alcoholics. Deep within, he knew that he needed some further insight for this special ministry to develop. How could he merge the meaningfulness of AA with the relevance of the Church?

For the answer, Grimm turned to further education. In June 1961 he began training to become a supervisor of clinical pastoral education. His training was supervised by Bill Currens, who was running an extended clinical pastoral education unit out of Lutheran Social Services in Minneapolis. Grimm assisted Currens one day a week by co-supervising a group of interns and by reading the written interviews of the students with the patients. He was also assigned the direction of one student under the guidance of Currens. At the same time, Grimm was organizing the pre-accreditation paperwork necessary to install a clinical pastoral education program at Willmar. He had to describe the goals of the program, the nature of the pastoral ministry, and the expectations for the students.

In the summer of 1963, Grimm became an acting supervisor of clinical pastoral education in alcoholism, and Willmar became an accredited site for training. Under the continued supervision of Currens, who came to Willmar one day a week to observe and counsel Grimm in his work, Grimm began to take students into Willmar's pastoral training program. He guided his students—both seminarians and ordained clergy—in how to respond both to the religious needs of believers and to the spiritual needs of the alcoholics, who included the indifferent, the atheist, and the agnostic. As Grimm gained his own insights into the fundamentals of pastoral care and the nature of alcoholism, he was better able to discern what he should be teaching his theological students. What they really needed to know and experience, he decided, was

1. The reality that alcoholics are not the same as mentally ill people.
2. The importance of prayer in the process of recovery. (Grimm never ceased to be amazed by the example of Bradley, the counselors, and others who prayed daily.)

3. The spirituality contained in Steps Two and Three of the AA program. (Grimm is the first to admit that, in those early days at Willmar, he did not fully understand the process of surrender. The recovering counselors urged him to read the writings of Harry Tiebout, assuring him that this psychiatrist "had a handle on the meaning of surrender for the alcoholic.")

4. The importance of honesty in the process of recovery. Alcoholics had to focus on themselves. If they were not being honest with themselves, they were not being honest with God.

Gordy Grimm—Hazelden's goodwill ambassador. Courtesy Hazelden-Pittman Archives

Grimm also sought to sensitize the clergy to an institutional environment that was indifferent, if not unfriendly, to religion and those who represented it. While most of his students were filled with apostolic zeal and believed that there was a message within the Christian faith that would move alcoholics, Grimm was shifting away from that ideal. He himself felt that while the religious message was true, alcoholics were not ready for it. It was not easy reconciling the Kingdom of God with the Fellowship of AA. His students had to understand that they could still help alcoholics recover even if they themselves had not reconciled the differences between the Church and AA.

While the challenge of implementing a clinical pastoral education program at Willmar stimulated Grimm, he also realized the hospital's multidisciplinary resources had been depleted. One by one, his mentors moved on to new challenges: Bradley and Rossi left for Lutheran General Hospital in Chicago in 1960, Anderson went to Hazelden in 1961, and Eiden retired the same year. The creative energies and enthusiasm that had marked the 1950s at Willmar had come to an end. In 1964, Anderson asked Grimm to come to Hazelden to organize a pastoral department and a training program for clergy. Grimm cleared it with his superiors and arrived there in January 1965. He remained for three productive decades.

Hazelden

Grimm discovered at Hazelden an environment that was truly receptive to the spiritual dimension of the AA program. For Pat Butler, Hazelden's founder and president as well as a devout Catholic, the Kingdom of God and the Fellowship of AA were not incompatible as he pursued his own recovery, and was actively involved in helping other alcoholics work through the accomodation between their recovery and their faith. Grimm found the spiritual atmosphere at Hazelden to be steeped in Catholicism. Lynn Carroll, the rehabilitation program director, considered it very important that people deal with the guilt and shame that they felt due to their alcoholism. Hazelden sought competent and knowledgeable clergy to help patients with the Fourth and Fifth Steps. One Catholic chaplain who heard Fifth Steps tried to invest everything spiritual with religious language and Catholic ritual. Pamphlets used by the patients to help them with their Fourth and Fifth Steps were framed in terms of the seven cardinal sins and of vices and virtues very unlike the instructions on the Fourth Step provided by the Big Book. When new meditation rooms were completed in 1966, Butler wanted them to serve as places where priests, while in treatment, could say Mass. One of the rooms contained a large crucifix.

Both Grimm and Anderson, himself a Catholic, were very uneasy with this distinctively Catholic flavor. Anderson believed that Jews and Protestants would not have anything to identify with. Grimm quickly discovered that, despite the presence of clergy, they had not been considered equal players with counselors in the treatment program at Hazelden. Both men can take credit for developing an ecumenical community more in keeping with the spirituality and ritual of AA. Anderson also had been hiring a host of professionals and giving them the freedom to create their roles on the multidisciplinary team. Grimm set to work defining the role of chaplains and ensuring their place as equal partners on that same team.

Carroll, himself a recovering alcoholic, served as Hazelden's guardian and protector of AA and its Steps. He feared the multidisciplinary team would undermine Hazelden's adherence to AA principles. When Grimm first arrived at Hazelden, Carroll brought him into his office, closed the door, and startled him by saying that Hazelden was "not big enough for the both of us." Needless to say, Grimm left the office somewhat unsettled.

The next week, Carroll had a change of heart. He had heard from Fred Eiden, who gave Grimm the green light with a very strong recommendation. Carroll then asked Grimm to meet with one of the patients who was both Jewish and an atheist. Grimm left that second encounter with Carroll relieved that he had been accepted by Mr. AA but anxious about the coming session with the atheist who was having a difficult time with the Higher Power concept. Grimm managed to convince the patient to keep an open mind and an initial acceptance of the group as his Higher Power.

At Hazelden Grimm came to a fuller understanding of the nature of alcoholism and the transformation involved in recovery. At Willmar this understanding had eluded him like a shadow under the water, never rising to the surface of his consciousness. Now he came to a heightened awareness of what Surrender, Powerlessness, and Higher Power really signified in the alcoholic's recovery process. He also got a handle on the meaning of self-centeredness, which according to the Big Book was the primary spiritual problem for the alcoholic. Grimm equated the AA concept of self-centeredness to the Christian understanding of false pride—the major obstacle to a right relationship with God.

The Pastoral Program

One of Grimm's first goals at Hazelden was to formalize the roles of the part-time clergy in the Pastoral Consultation Program. The consultants who were employed were very uneven in their pastoral understanding and implementation of the work for which they were hired. It was not unusual for one of them to fall asleep while hearing the Fifth Steps of the patients. Another would never vary from doing eight a day, and a convoy of patients would march in and out on an hourly basis. Besides, there never seemed to be enough clergy on hand to meet the needs of all the patients. Grimm provided structure, consistency, and direction for these activities. Contracts were signed with select clergy to spend one day a week at Hazelden doing family counseling, hearing Fourth and Fifth Steps, attending staff meetings, and lecturing. They were paid according to their skill, ability, and involvement.

Grimm made certain that those he hired and those who went through training understood and accepted the ascetical and spiritual foundations of AA:

1. The recognition of a Higher Power.
2. The conversion, or transformation, process through the surrender that occurs within the individual.
3. The striving for moral integrity and the restoration of relationships with self, others, and a Higher Power as the core of this spiritual conversion.
4. The need for ascetical practices for recovering people to nourish their spiritual lives.
5. The practice of good works through service to others in need.

Grimm was able to comprehend AA's nondogmatic, nonmoralistic approach to addiction, which views the alcoholic as a sick person in need of healing, not a bad person in need of repentance. He emphasized for those under his supervision that the stress should be upon the removal of character defects rather than upon forgiveness of sin.

Within this context, pastoral care providers became co-sojourners with the patients on their journey to recovery. Clergy people listened to the stories, struggles, strengths, and weaknesses of those in recovery and developed a spiritual assessment to add to other information and data gathered for the individual treatment plan. In this way, the clergy person soon had a role in the overall assessment process. The spiritual and the behavioral often looked very much alike, and at times it was difficult to sort out the differences in the assessments of the counselor, the chaplain, and the psychologist.

Gradually, at the request of the counselors, the clergy began to orient the patients to the Second and Third Steps. It became clear to all the staff involved in the treatment process that grief was an outstanding issue, especially for women, and had to be dealt with in treatment to help ensure sobriety afterward. Grimm invited Howard Clinebell, the recognized expert on dealing with grief in those days, to come and give a series of workshops for clergy and for the rest of the counseling staff. Clinebell emphasized that while there are universals in the grieving process, there also is an individual uniqueness; while there can be a general understanding of the grieving process, that does not automatically guarantee the clergy person a formula that fits all.

Grimm sought to make the approach to spirituality very concrete, specific, and oriented toward change, growth, and fulfillment. Addiction, viewed spiritually, is a very deep, dark hole; a form of slavery; a turning away from life toward death. What begins as a yearning for transcendence and ecstasy slips into loss of control in the use of chemicals and ends in complete demoralization and despair. Spiritually, the clients who seek help at Hazelden have experienced the worst. This "hitting bottom" triggers the need to change. Through group support and affirmation, patients learn how to support a life of sobriety and serenity. The acceptance of the Second and Third Steps—"coming to believe" (Step Two) and "making a decision to turn our lives and our wills over to the care of God as we understand him" (Step Three)—represents a major transformation in the life of the chemically dependent person. Patients must come to believe that they not only can deal with their chronic condition but also can initiate those changes that are necessary to meet life's challenges. Under Grimm's guidance, the clergy explored the meaning of these Steps with the patients and clarified with examples the important principle of "God working through people."

Grimm's early struggles at Willmar trying to define his own role and the role of the pastoral counselor finally came to fruition during his first decade at Hazelden. He had learned how to help the alcoholic, and he could transmit what he had integrated for himself to the students who came to participate in the clinical pastoral education program.

Clinical Pastoral Education

Though Grimm struggled at Willmar and initially at Hazelden with what clinical pastoral students needed to learn about helping alcoholics, the concept of clinical pastoral education had actually gotten its start in the mid-1920s. From its informal beginnings, clinical pastoral education had undergone quite an evolution. In the first stage, clergy students searched for an answer to the question: "What must I *do* to be of help to the patient?" In the second stage, from about 1935 to 1945, the question was: "What must I *know* to be of help to the patient?" During that period students were required to draw up exhaustive histories of the patients' backgrounds. In the following decade the emphasis shifted to: "What must I *say* to be of help to the patient?" It was at this point that counseling and verbatims emerged as the most important aspects of the training. By the early 1960s, the final and contemporary stage had begun to emerge. Drawing from the wisdom accrued from the three previous stages, students now seek answers to the questions: "What must I *know, experience, and understand about myself* to better help the patient?" Grimm profited from this development in clinical pastoral education as he sought to establish his own program.

In 1966, the Lutheran Council, USA, accredited Grimm's clinical pastoral education program at Hazelden. By 1968, Grimm and his staff were conducting two formal sessions a year. Initially, each session lasted three months. His vision was to train the clergy to understand first of all themselves and secondly the nature of the disease and how to help chemically dependent people through the Twelve Steps of AA.

Trainees started out the session in a treatment unit, learning about the patients. Then they participated in a multidisciplinary treatment team, in which each member worked to reach the patient from the perspective of a specific discipline. Students experienced the challenge and opportunity of sharing their expertise with the treatment team. The form and depth of the participation of the professionals in the care of the patient depended a great deal on the attitude and vision of the supervisors of the units. Some were autocratic and some were very collegial in their appreciation of other team members. Thus the role and involvement of the pastoral trainees on the treatment team depended very much on the attitude of the supervisor. During their training, students also attended seminars, read extensively, and went on field trips, all of which were geared to raise their sensitivity to chemical dependency. In time, the length of the training increased to a year-long residential program, and Grimm added other components, such as group analysis of individual counseling techniques, role playing, and critiques of lectures.

Grimm and his staff proved themselves expert at helping students gain knowledge about themselves and insights into how they related to others. During discussions about their verbatims, the students never ceased to admire Grimm's incisive comments about them and their pastoral activities. Nevertheless, many of the businessmen on the board questioned the value of the clinical pastoral education program because it did not pay for itself. Some members objected to the idea and image of Hazelden as a theological seminary. Anderson, however, convinced Pat Butler that clinical pastoral education was a worthwhile investment for the impact that Hazelden would have throughout the country. For years, Hazelden's clinical pastoral education program was a model in the United States and the preeminent training center for clergy who worked in recovery settings.

New Responsibilities

In addition to pastoral care and clergy training, Grimm was also responsible for the Professionals in Residence Program, begun in 1972. It was initiated in conjunction with the Minnesota State Department of Education as a one-week workshop for members of the Minnesota Educators Association. In 1975, Grimm became the director of the newly formed Training Division, which encompassed the programs already in place for training counselors, clergy, and professionals. Under Grimm's leadership, the Professionals in Residence program expanded to include a wide range of professionals, including medical doctors and interns. More than 500 graduates from the counselor training program have practiced their profession in thirty-three countries. More than 240 clergy from around the world participated in the clinical pastoral education program during its years of operation, from 1966 to 1992.

Grimm continued to defend the role of clergy on the multidisciplinary team after Hazelden received accreditation from the Joint Commission on the Accreditation of Hospitals. This had a huge impact on the Minnesota Model—most especially on pastoral care. The Hazelden model of treatment up to that point had never been a medical model. Treatment was not provided in a hospital setting, and doctors did not administer the treatment program. While the medical aspect of the illness, namely detoxication, was necessary, it was not the primary focus of treatment. The Joint Commission was accustomed to accrediting hospitals, in which the role of a chaplain was not really integrated into the medical care that it provided. Spiritual concerns were not considered an essential part of medical treatment. Grimm, however, insisted that pastoral care continue to play a very important, integrated role in the Hazelden model. He noted that the spirituality of the Twelve Step program was not the same as the religious practice provided by a hospital chaplain, who stood on the outside looking in at the hospital-medical model. Nevertheless, with accreditation the expectation to be as efficient as possible was so dominant that at one point Grimm thought about pulling pastoral care out of the multidisciplinary team because the spiritual assessment appeared so superficial alongside detoxication and the physical, psychological, and social assessments. The principle of efficiency distracted the professional team from its ultimate task—the care of patients. Grimm encouraged other members of the multidisciplinary team to remember this larger goal.

Under Grimm and Anderson, prevention became a principal thrust of Hazelden's efforts in the 1980s. Both men were instrumental in gaining the support of Joan Kroc to finance the construction of the Cork Center, in which the Prevention and Health Promotion departments would be lodged. In 1984 Grimm became the director of Health Promotion.

From 1988 until his retirement in 1995, Grimm's role continued to broaden, as he became responsible for public policy, development, and research. He regretted being pulled further away from the work that he loved the best—pastoral care and pastoral training; eventually, he had to relinquish supervision of those areas. He was deeply pained by the closure of the clinical pastoral education program in 1992. For many clinical pastoral education alumni as well as for Grimm, the program defined the spiritual character of Hazelden. Yet the Pastoral Department and its clergy still maintain

The groundbreaking of the Cork Center at Hazelden in Center City, Minnesota. Pictured from left to right are Gordy Grimm, Gerald Rauenhorst, Joan Kroc, Dan Anderson, and Harry Swift. Courtesy Hazelden-Pittman Archives

a very important role as part of the multidisciplinary team, a legacy from Grimm that continues to thrive.

Retirement

Grimm retired in the spring of 1995, thirty years after he came to Hazelden. His contributions to the field have been enormous. Well-known and respected in the field of chemical dependency, he has given graciously of himself to others. Grimm takes great pride in his contributions to clinical pastoral education and to the evolution of the Minnesota Model, making pastoral care professionals part of the multidisciplinary team.

Yet he takes even greater pride in his family and the support that they have been to him over the years. He and his wife, Esther, have welcomed into the warmth of their home many people on journeys similar to their own. The two met in 1958 at Willmar State Hospital, where they both worked at the time, she as a nurse in charge of women alcoholics. He was attracted to Esther's smile, her laughter, her warm welcoming and nurturing personality. She also had an intuitive understanding of the nature of alcoholism—gained through childhood as well as professional experiences. Together, they have given and received much from their three children. John's listening skills and Mary's gentle nature serve as continual reminders of two of Grimm's most important pastoral skills. Jim, the youngest, suffers from cerebral palsy that has left him both nonambulatory and nonverbal. Those who visit the Grimm home and make Jim's acquaintance come away with a new definition of wholeness. Behind and beyond the physical handicap is a courageous spirit that few of us will ever be asked to demonstrate.

Throughout the world, the people Grimm has influenced regard him as their mentor and friend. His influence went far beyond the graduates of his training programs. Wherever he traveled, he touched communities with his spiritual message about alcoholism and the values of integrity and honesty. In a very real way, Hazelden's new Meditation Center, built in 2001, is a visible symbol of the spiritual dimension of Hazelden's services to the recovery community—a testimony to what Grimm brought to the Minnesota Model.

Author's note

Though Grimm was a powerful communicator, he was not a writer. He did not publish anything; rather, he influenced people through direct speech and through deed. The following appendices give a small sampling of the pastoral environment in which Grimm worked. The lecture schedules demonstrate the educational component of treatment at Willmar, 1961–1962. The "Guide to Fourth Step Inventory" is but one example of the Christian-Catholic flavor of some of the practices, e.g., the Fourth Step preparation, which existed at Hazelden when Dan Anderson and Grimm arrived. Both of them succeeded in changing these decidedly religious practices. The transcription of one of Grimm's Fifth Step lectures demonstrates Grimm at his finest, ministering to the spiritual needs of those suffering from alcoholism and chemical dependency.

Willmar State Hospital
Inebriate Orientation Schedule
November 13 to December 29, 1961

The following schedule of Orientation Meetings will begin on Monday, November 13th, and will continue as indicated. Meetings are in the AA Room and will start at 8:00 A.M. and end at 8:50 A.M.

Mon.	Nov. 13	Introduction	Dr. S. Vertuca
Tues.	Nov. 14	FILM: "Alcohol and the Human Body"	Dr. L. A. Smith
Wed.	Nov. 15	Medical Symptoms of Alcoholism	Dr. L. A. Smith
Thurs.	Nov. 16	MOVIE: "House of Cards"	
Fri.	Nov. 17	Symptoms & Progress of Alcoholism I	Mr. R. Selvig
Mon.	Nov. 20	Symptoms & Progress of Alcoholism II	Mr. R. Selvig
Tues.	Nov. 21	Mental Mechanisms I	Dr. J. T. Laird
Wed.	Nov. 22	Mental Mechanisms II	Dr. J. T. Laird
Thurs.	Nov. 23	HOLIDAY	
Fri.	Nov. 24	The Church and Alcoholism	Rev. Kauffman
Mon.	Nov. 27	Spiritual Aspects of Rehabilitation	Rev. Kauffman
Tues.	Nov. 28	FILM: "Problem Drinkers"	
Wed.	Nov. 29	Ignorance, Learning, and Application	Mr. P. Paulding
Thurs.	Nov. 30	Danger Signals	Mr. F. Eiden
Fri.	Dec. 1	The AA Way of Life	Mr. R. Selvig
Mon.	Dec. 4	Rehabilitation (psychological, physical, social)	Dr. V. Behrendt
Tues.	Dec. 5	Psychiatric Problems of Alcoholics	Dr. V. Behrendt
Wed.	Dec. 6	Content & Importance of AA Meetings	Mr. M. Johnson

Thurs.	Dec. 7	Resolving Personal Conflicts	Mr. R. Selvig
Fri.	Dec. 8	Fellowship Club & the Alcoholic	Mr. McAllister Gordon or Mr. Richard Lynch
Mon.	Dec. 11	Personality Characteristics of Alcoholics	Mr. R. Selvig
Tues.	Dec. 12	Steps Four and Five	Rev. G. Grimm
Wed.	Dec. 13	Characteristics of Addiction	Mr. P. Paulding
Thurs.	Dec. 14	Psychology of Alcoholism I	Mr. F. Eiden
Fri.	Dec. 15	Psychology of Alcoholism II	Mr. F. Eiden
Mon.	Dec. 18	Pastoral Counseling and Families	Rev. G. Grimm
Tues.	Dec. 19	Communication Patterns of Alcoholics	Dr. J. T. Laird
Wed.	Dec. 20	Hospital & Community Resources and Marital Problems of Alcoholics	Mr. H. Swift, MSW
Thurs.	Dec. 21	Does AA Provide You with What You Want?	Mr. F. Eiden
Fri.	Dec. 22	FILM: "I Am An Alcoholic"	
Mon.	Dec. 25	HOLIDAY	
Tues.	Dec. 26	MOVIE: "David, Profile of Problem Drinkers"	
Wed.	Dec. 27	MOVIE: "Alcoholism" and "To Your Health"	
Thurs.	Dec. 28	MOVIE: "House of Cards"	
Fri.	Dec. 29	Summary	Dr. S. Vertuca

Willmar State Hospital
Inebriate Orientation Schedule
July 3 to August 10, 1962

The following schedule of Orientation Meetings will begin on Tuesday, July 3rd, and will continue as indicated. Meetings are held in the Auditorium beginning at 8:00 A.M.

Tues.	July 3	FILM: "Alcohol and the Human Body"	Dr. R. Heilman
Wed.	July 4	HOLIDAY	
Thurs.	July 5	Who Is An Alcoholic?	Dr. R. Heilman
Fri.	July 6	Symptoms & Progress of Alcoholism I	Mr. F. Norstrom
Mon.	July 9	Symptoms & Progress of Alcoholism II	Mr. F. Norstrom
Tues.	July 10	Personality Characteristics of Alcoholics I	Mr. R. Selvig
Wed.	July 11	Personality Characteristics of Alcoholics II	Mr. R. Selvig
Thurs.	July 12	Mental Mechanisms	Dr. J. T. Laird
Fri.	July 13	Marital & Family Problems of the Alcoholic I	Mr. H. Swift, MSW
Mon.	July 16	Marital & Family Problems of the Alcoholic II	Mr. H. Swift, MSW
Tues.	July 17	Resolving Personal Conflicts	Mr. R. Selvig
Wed.	July 18	Ignorance, Learning & Application	Mr. P. Paulding
Thurs.	July 19	Communication Patterns of Alcoholics	Dr. J. T. Laird
Fri.	July 20	Rehabilitation (psychological, physical, social)	Mr. H. Swift, MSW
Mon.	July 23	Psychiatric Problems of Alcoholism	Dr. S. Vertuca
Tues.	July 24	Danger Signals	Mr. P. Paulding

Wed.	July 25	The AA Way of Life	Mr. A. Iverson
Thurs.	July 26	Content & Importance of AA Meetings	Mr. M. Johnson
Fri.	July 27	Fellowship Club & the Alcoholic	Mr. Richard Lynch
Mon.	July 30	Steps Four and Five of AA	Rev. G. Grimm
Tues.	July 31	Psychology of Alcoholism I	Dr. S. Vertuca
Wed.	Aug. 1	Psychology of Alcoholism II	Dr. S. Vertuca
Thurs.	Aug. 2	Characteristics of Addiction	Mr. P. Paulding
Fri.	Aug. 3	The Church & Alcoholism	Rev. J. Kauffman
Mon.	Aug. 6	Spiritual Aspects of Rehabilitation	Rev. J. Kauffman
Tues.	Aug. 7	Sponsorship in AA	Mr. G. Farmer
Wed.	Aug. 8	Does AA Provide You With What You Want?	Mr. G. Farmer
Thurs.	Aug. 9	FILM: "I Am An Alcoholic"	
Fri.	Aug. 10	FILM: "David, Profile of Problem Drinkers"	

Guide to Fourth Step Inventory
Hazelden Foundation, 1961

In making the Inventory, we need to examine ourselves in the following:

A. The 10 Commandments
B. The 7 Cardinal Sins
C. Personality Defects
D. Virtues, Attitudes, and Responsibilities

The procedure could be as follows:

1. An exhaustive and honest consideration of the above, applying these to our past and present.
2. Omit nothing because of shame, embarrassment, or fear. The easiest start is, "What is the worst thing I have ever done?"
3. Determine particularly the attitudes, desires, and motivations that plague me.
4. Write the Inventory down. We want to meet this face to face. If you wish to destroy it afterwards, do so.
5. List both assets and liabilities. We will rebuild on our assets, such as:
   a. Knowing right from wrong.
   b. We are good hearted and like people.
   c. We want to do the right thing.
   d. We hate ourselves for our wrongs and our failures.

A. The Ten Commandments

1. I am the Lord, thy God, thou shalt not have strange gods before me.
   Is God omnipotent to me or are my gods money, fame, position? Does He come first, or do I? Do I seek His will?

2. Thou shalt not take the name of the Lord, thy God, in vain.
Am I profane and would I be to God's face? Isn't that pretty phony respect?
3. Remember to keep holy the Sabbath Day.
Would my attitude towards "religion" and church perpetuate spirituality?
4. Honor thy father and thy mother.
The law of love, respect, and obedience. Have I as a parent earned that honor?
5. Thou shalt not kill.
Here include hate, anger, resentment, and hurt through our misdeeds.
6. Thou shalt not commit adultery.
Not alone immoral acts but the thinking, temporising, and condoning as well. The mental, emotional, and spiritual misery I imposed on myself and others.
7. Thou shalt not steal.
How about cheating, misrepresenting, pressure deals, debts, etc?
8. Thou shalt not bear false witness against thy neighbor.
Include slander, gossip, and using dubious testimony.
9. Thou shalt not covet thy neighbor's wife.
Have we violated another's marriage under any circumstances?
10. Thou shalt not covet thy neighbor's goods.
Remember envy, competitive dishonesty, "dog eat dog" tactics.

B. The 7 Cardinal Sins

PRIDE—Egotistical vanity—too great admiration of one's self. Pride makes me my own law, judge of morality, and my own God. Pride produces criticism, backbiting, slander, barbed words, and character assassinations which elevate my own ego. Pride makes me condemn as fools those who criticize me. Pride gives me excuses. Pride produces:

1. Boasting—or self glorification
2. Love of publicity—conceit in what others say about me

3. Hypocrisy—pretending to be what I am not
4. Hardheadness—refusal to give up my own will
5. Discord—resenting any who cross me
6. Quarrelsomeness—quarreling whenever another challenges my wishes
7. Disobedience—refusal to submit my will to the will of lawful superiors and to God's will

COVETOUSNESS OR AVARICE—Perversion of man's God given right to own things. Do I desire wealth in the form of money or other things as an end in itself rather than as a means to an end, such as taking care of the soul and body in their needs? In acquiring wealth in any form, do I disregard the rights of others? Am I dishonest, and if so to what degree and in what fashion? Do I give an honest day's work for an honest day's pay, for example? How do I use what I have? Am I stingy with my family? Do I love money or possessions for these things *in themselves?* How excessive is my love of luxury? How do I preserve my wealth or increase it? Do I stoop to such devices as fraud or perjury or dishonesty or sharp practices in dealing with others? Do I try to fool myself in these regards? Do I call stinginess, thrift? Do I call questionable business, Big Business or drive? Do I call unreasonable hoarding, security? If I presently have no money and little other wealth, how and by what practice will I go about getting it later? Will I do almost anything to attain these things and kid myself by tagging my methods with innocent names?

LUST—Inordinate love and desires of the pleasures of the flesh. Am I guilty of lust in any of its forms? Do I tell myself that improper or undue indulgence in sex activities is required for "good health" or needed for a full life or as a basic requirement for "self-expression"? Do I engage in any kind of sex activity out of wedlock? If married, do I act like a man or a beast? Do I really believe that lust is love, or do I secretly know that lust is not love, and love is not sex? Don't I know that sex is only one of the expressions of love, morally limited to wedlock? Have I engaged in any kind of lustful excesses that have affected my reason by:

1. Perverting my understanding and making me intellectually blind and unable to see the truth?
2. Weakening my prudence, and thereby harming my sense of values and causing rashness?
3. Building up self-love, and so generating thoughtlessness?
4. Weakening my will until I have lost the power of decision and have become a man of inconstant character?

Does God, as I understand Him, really do anything for a man who is sexually loose either in wedlock or out? Would He approve of my sex habits?

ENVY—Sadness at another's good. How envious a man am I? Do I dislike seeing others happy or successful as though they had taken from my happiness or success? Do I resent those smarter than I am because I am jealous? Do I ever criticize the good done by others because I secretly wish I'd done it myself for the honor or prestige to be gained? Am I ever envious enough to try to lower another's reputation by starting or engaging in gossip about him? Do I ever carry tales? Being envious includes calling religious people "hypocrites" because they go to church and try to be religiously good even though subject to human failings even as I am. Am I guilty here? Do I deprecate the well-bred man by saying or feeling that he puts on airs? Do I ever accuse the educated or wise or learned of being high brow because I envy their advantages? Do I genuinely love other people or do I find them distasteful, because I envy them in the above ways or other ways?

ANGER—A violent desire to punish others. Do I ever fly into rages of temper, become revengeful, entertain urges to "get even" or an "I'll not let him get away with it" attitude? Do I ever resort to violence, ever clinch fists, or stomp about in a temper flare up? Am I touchy, unduly sensitive, impatient at the least slight? Do I ever murmur or grumble even in small matters? Do I ignore the fact that anger prevents development of personality, and halts spiritual progress? Do I realize at all times that anger disrupts mental poise and often ruins good judgment? Do I permit anger to rule me when I know it blinds me to the rights of others? How can I excuse even small tantrums of temper when anger destroys the spirit of recollection which I need for compliance with the inspirations of God? Do I permit myself to become angry when others are weak and become angry with me? Can I hope to entertain the serene spirit of God within a soul often beset by angry flare ups of even minor importance?

GLUTTONY—Abuse of lawful pleasures God attached to eating and drinking of foods required for self preservation. Do I weaken my moral and intellectual life by excessive use of food and drink? Do I generally eat to excess and thus enslave my soul and character to the pleasures of the body beyond reasonable needs of the body? Do I kid myself I can be a "hog" without affecting my moral life? Did I ever, when drinking, become nauseated and disgorge only to immediately return and drink some more? What about my drinking before alcoholic drinking set in? Did I drink so much that my intellect and personality deteriorated; so much that memory, judgment, and concentration were affected; so much that personal pride and social judgment vanished; so much that I developed a spirit of despair; a weakening of my will and materialization of life as opposed to the spiritualization?

SLOTH—Illness of the will which causes a neglect of duty. Am I lazy, given to idleness, procrastination, nonchalance, and indifference in material things? Am I lukewarm in Prayer? Do I hold self-discipline in contempt? Would I rather read a novel than study something requiring brain work, the Big Book, for example? Am I faint hearted in performance of those things which are morally or spiritually difficult? Am I ever listless with aversion to effort in any form? Am I easily distracted from things spiritual, quickly turning to things temporal? Am I ever indolent to the extent that I perform work carelessly?

C. Personality Defects

When an alcoholic wishes to make Step #4 in AA, he looks for his own assets and his own defects. Assets were briefly discussed on page #1. Enlarge on them and list them on paper. On defects, he generally finds some or all of the following, in varying degrees, in himself:

1. Selfishness
2. Alibis
3. Dishonest thinking (akin to lying)
4. Pride
5. Resentment (under Anger in the 7 Cardinal Sins)
6. Intolerance
7. Impatience
8. Envy (listed in the 7 Cardinal Sins)
9. Phonyness
10. Procrastination
11. Self pity
12. Feelings easily hurt
13. Fear

1. *Selfishness:* (ego-centric) Def. Taking care of one's own comfort, advantage, etc., without regard for the interest of others.
    a. (Example) The family would like an outing. Dad would like drinking, golf, fishing, or just has a hangover. Who wins?
    b. (Example) Child needs a new pair of shoes. Our hero puts it off till pay day, but gets himself a fifth the same night. Unselfish?
    c. Ego-centric: Feels the world revolves around him. Afraid

to dance because he might appear awkward. Fears to appear at a disadvantage in any venture because it might injure his "false front" to people.

2. *Alibis:* The highly developed art of justifying our drinking and behavior through mental gymnastics. Excuses for drinking—the alcoholic calls them reasons. Phony as a $3.00 bill. Check these; add your own:

a. A few will straighten me out.

b. Starting tomorrow, I'm going to change.

c. If I didn't have a wife and family.

d. If it wasn't for my mother-in-law.

e. If I could start all over again.

f. A little drinking will allow me to think.

g. Might as well get drunk; I'm no good for anything else today.

h. If some people didn't get on my nerves.

i. If I had only done things differently.

j. (And on and on and on. We can always come up with the right answer).

3. *Dishonest Thinking:* Another way of lying. We may even take truths or facts as our hypothesis and then through some phony mental hop-scotch, come up with exactly the conclusions we had planned to arrive at. Boy, we are beauts at that business. No wonder we drink!

a. My secret love life is going to raise the roof if I drop her. It is not fair to burden my wife with that sort of knowledge. Therefore, I will hang on to my babe. This mess isn't her fault. (Good, solid con.)

b. If I tell my family about the $500.00 bonus, it will all go for old bills, clothes, dentist, etc. I've got to have some drinking money. Why start a family argument? Leave well enough alone.

c. My wife dresses well; eats well; the kids are getting a good education. What more do they want?

4. *Pride:* One of the 7 Cardinal Sins and a serious character defect. Def: Egotistical vanity—too great admiration of one's self. Inordinate self-esteem, arrogance, ostentatious display, bragging.
   a. You are ashamed to let people know you had quit drinking.
   b. You make a mistake and are called on it. What reaction? Do you burn?
   c. Does your pride suffer when you admit you can't handle alcohol?
   d. Pride makes me my own law, my own judge of morality, and my own god.
   e. Pride produces criticism, back biting slander and character assassination.
   f. Pride makes me make excuses for my own mistakes, because I cannot admit I made a mistake.
5. *Resentment:* Under *Anger* in the 7 Cardinal Sins and, for many alcoholics, the most damning fault in the entire repertoire. It is the displeasure aroused by a real or imagined wrong or injury, accompanied with irritation, exasperation or hate.
   a. You are fired from your job; therefore you hate the boss.
   b. Sister warns you about excessive drinking. You get fighting mad at her.
   c. Co-worker is doing a good job and gets the accolades. You have a drinking record and fear he may be promoted over you. You hate his guts.
   d. You may have a resentment towards a person, a group of people (nationalities), may resent or hate institutions, religions, be a KKK, etc.

Anger and resentment lead to bickering, friction, hatred, unjust revenge, alienation of the children. It brings out the worst of our immaturity and produces misery to ourselves and all concerned.

6. *Intolerance:* Def: Refusal to put up with beliefs (religious or political), practices, customs, or habits that differ from our own.

   a. Do we hate other people because they are Jews, Negroes, Indians or because they have a different religion or nationality than ours?

   b. Did we have any choice in being born white, black, yellow, or copper colored? What would you do if you were black—hang yourself?

   c. Similarly, isn't our religion usually "inherited"?

7. *Impatience:* Def: Unwillingness to bear delay, opposition, pain, bother, etc. calmly.

   a. An alcoholic is a person who jumps on a horse and gallops off madly in all directions at the same time.

   b. Do we blow our stack when our wife keeps us waiting a few minutes over the "alloted time" we gave her? Did she ever have to wait for us?

8. *Envy:* Also included in the 7 Cardinal Sins. Def: Sadness at another's good fortune.

   a. Guy across the street buys a new car each year. Makes us look bad because he saves his money and can afford it. So we ridicule him to save face.

   b. Brother-in-law is a family man, hard worker, decent type. We're naturally envious, consider him stuffed shirt, holier than thou type.

   c. The old familiar: "If I only had that guy's chances everything would have been all right."

9. *Phonyness:* A manifestation of our great false pride; a form of lying; rank and brash dishonesty. It's the old false front.

   a. I present my wife with a new car as evidence of my love. Just by pure coincidence, it helped smooth over my last disastrous binge.

   b. I buy a new suit because my business position demands it

(I tell myself). Meanwhile, the family also could use both food and clothes.

   c. The joker who enthralls an AA audience with his profound wisdom but hasn't got the time of day for his wife and kids. Great guy at a meeting, but a boor and a tyrant at home. Our hero.

   d. When we stop and think it over, just how smelly can we get?

10. *Procrastination.* Def: Putting off . . . postponing things that need to be done . . . the familiar "I'll do it tomorrow."

   a. Did little jobs, put off, become big and nigh impossible later? Did that contribute to my drinking because my problems piled up?

   b. Do I self-pamper myself by doing things "my way" or do I attempt to put order and discipline into my daily duties?

   c. Can I handle little jobs I am asked to take care of or do I feel picked upon; or am I just too lazy or proud?

   d. Little things, done for the love of God, make them great.

11. *Self Pity:* An insidious personality defect and a danger signal to look for. Stop it in a hurry—it's the build-up for a drunk.

   a. These people at the party are having fun with their drinking. Why can't I be like that? (The aforementioned is the long version of "Woe is me.")

   b. If I had that guy's money, I wouldn't have any worries.

   c. P.S. When you feel that way, visit an alcoholic ward, cancer ward, or children's hospital and then count your blessings.

12. *Feelings Easily Hurt:* Sensitive, touchy, thin-skinned.

   a. I walk down the street and say Hello to someone. He doesn't answer. I'm hurt and mad. It was *me* he snubbed—that's all that counts. I am all "shook up." Real maturity there, old boy.

   b. I am expecting to be called on at my AA meeting but the

MC forgets it. I imagine all sorts of things in my upset state and conclude the MC doesn't like me. That's a dirty trick, and I'll get even with him.

13. *Fear:* An inner forboding, real or imagined, of doom ahead. We suspect our drinking, overt acts, negligence, etc. is catching up with us. We fear the worst.

    a. When we learn to accept (Step #1), ask God's help, and face ourselves, with honesty, the nightmare of fear will be gone.

Time Out

If you have gone through the outline to this point without coming up for air—it figures. We did our drinking the same way. Whoa, boy—easy does it.

Take this in reasonable stages. Assimilate each portion thoughtfully. The reading of this is important—the application, 10 times more so. Take some time now for a hike, horseshoes, T.V., etc., and let this settle and apply it into some sort of workable daily plan. Work it for a day or two. Then come back for the rest of it.

D. Virtues, Attitudes, and Responsibilities

When the alcoholic stops drinking, part of his life is taken away from him. This is a terrible loss to sustain, unless it is replaced. We can't just boot drinking out the window—drinking meant too much to us: the means to face life; the key to escape; the tool for our problems. So, in approaching a new way of life, a new set of tools are substituted—the 12 Steps and the AA way of life.

The same principle applies in eliminating our character defects. We replace them through employing substitutions better adapted to good living. As with drinking, you don't fight the defects—you *replace* them.

Use the following for further character analysis but also as a guide to character building, as well—these are the new tools. The objective is neither sainthood or the All-American. We will be happy with the type of living that produces self respect, respect and love of others, and security from the nightmare of compulsive drinking.

1. *The Divine Virtues—Faith, Hope, and Charity*
   a. *Faith:* The act of leaving that part of our destiny we cannot control (i.e., our future) to the care of a Power greater than ourselves, or God, with assurance that it will work out for our well being. Shaky, at first, it becomes a deep conviction.
      (1) Faith is a gift but one acquired through application: acceptance, daily prayer, daily meditation and our own effort.
      (2) We depend on faith. We have faith that dinner will be served, that the car will start, that our co-workers will handle their end. If we had no faith, we would come apart at the seams.
      (3) Spiritual faith is the accepting of our gifts, limitations, problems and trials with equal gratitude, knowing God has His plan for us. With "Thy will be done" as our daily guide, we will lose our fear, find ourselves, find our destiny.
   b. *Hope:* Faith suggests reliance: "We came to believe . . . ." Hope assumes faith but also aims for objectives. We hope for sobriety, for self respect, for love of family. Hope resolves itself into a driving force; it gives purpose to our daily living.
      (1) Faith gives us direction; Hope, the head of steam.
      (2) Hope reflects attitude. Remove hope and our attitude becomes insipid.
   c. *Charity:* "So there abide faith, hope and charity, these three; but the greatest of these is charity."
      (1) "Charity is patient, is kind; charity does not envy, is

not pretentious, is not puffed up, is not ambitious, is not self seeking, is not provoked; thinks no evil, does not rejoice over wickedness, but rejoices with the truth; bears with all things, believes all things, hopes all things, endures all things . . . " (1 Cor. 13:1–13)

(2) In its deeper sense, charity is the art of living realistically and fully, guided by spiritual awareness of our responsibilities and our debt of gratitude to Almighty God and to others.

Analysis: Have I utilized the qualities of Faith, Hope, and Charity in my past living. How would they apply to my new way of life?

2. *The Little Virtues—The Building Material*
   a. *Courtesy*—Some of us are actually afraid to be gentlemen. We'd rather be boors, self-pampering type.
   b. *Cheerfulness*—Circumstances don't determine our frame of mind. We do. Today I will be cheerful. I will look for the beauty in life.
   c. *Order*—Live today only; organize this day. Order is the first law of Heaven.
   d. *Loyalty*—The test of a man's sense of obligation.
   e. *Use of time*—Time can be productive, abused, or desecrated.
   f. *Punctuality*—Self discipline; order; consideration for others.
   g. *Sincerity*—The mark of self respect and genuineness. Sincerity carries conviction, generates enthusiasm, is contagious.
   h. *Caution in speech*—Watch thy erring member, the tongue. We can be vicious or thoughtless. Too often the damage is irreparable.
   i. *Kindness*—One of life's great satisfactions. We haven't

known real happiness until we have given of ourselves. Practice daily.

j. *Patience*—The antidote to resentments, self pity, impulsiveness.

k. *Tolerance*—Requires common courtesy, courage, live and let live.

l. *Integrity*—The ultimate qualification of a man; honest, loyal, sincere.

m. *Balance*—Don't take yourself too seriously. We get better perspective if we can laugh at ourselves. It will cure the piques.

n. *Gratitude*—The man without gratitude is stupid, arrogant or both. Gratitude is simply honest recognition of help received. Use it in our prayers, 12th Step work, our family relationship.

Analysis: In considering the Little Virtues, where did I fail particularly and how did that contribute to my accumulated problem? What virtues should I pay attention to in this rebuilding problem?

Have I used these at home and with those that love me?

How about starting NOW, applying little acts of consideration, unselfishness, and gratitude today? Don't make a production out of it; 3 or 4 little acts every day is far better than running the gamut one day and "resting up" the next.

3. *Just for Today—A Plan for Living*

a. A beautifully designed plan of action to handle *Today*. Don't let its simplicity fool you. This hits us where we used to live.

b. Live one day at a time; handle our drinking problem for today, only. Yesterday's gone; tomorrow may not come. Today is ours.

Just for Today I will try to live through this day only and not tackle my whole life problem at once. I can do something for twelve hours that would appall me if I felt that I had to keep it up for a lifetime.

Just for Today I will be happy. This assumes to be true what Abraham Lincoln said, that, "Most folks are as happy as they make up their minds to be."

Just for Today I will adjust myself to what is, and not try to adjust everything to my own desires. I will take my luck as it comes, and fit myself to it.

Just for Today I will strengthen my mind. I will study. I will learn something useful. I will not be a mental loafer. I will read something that requires effort, thought, and concentration.

Just for Today I will exercise my soul in three ways: I will do somebody a good turn, and not get found out; if anybody knows of it, it will not count. I will do at least two things I don't want to do—just for exercise. I will not show anyone that my feelings are hurt; they may be hurt, but today I will not show it.

Just for Today I will have a program. I may not follow it exactly, but I will have it. I will save myself from two pests: hurry and indecision.

Just for Today I will have a quiet half hour all by myself, and relax. During this half hour, some time, I will try to get a better perspective of my life.

Just for Today I will be unafraid. Especially I will not be afraid to enjoy what is beautiful, and to believe that as I give to the world, so the world will give to me.

Just for Today I will be agreeable. I will look as well as I can, dress becomingly, talk low, act courteously, criticize not one bit, not find fault with anything and try not to improve or regulate anybody except myself.

4. *Attitudes*
   a. *To God*
      (1) Have I based my concept (or refusal) of God principally through my early training, hearsay, disappointments, or emotional approaches? Would I prepare for

a career or even a hobby in the same manner? In other words, have I sought God?

(2) Do I appreciate the magnitude of the spiritual as applied to:
(a) My daily living?
(b) My problems, frustrations, despair, bitterness, and boredom?
(c) My present mess? Can I accept God's judgment as better than my own?

(3) Conceding the possible importance of spiritual development, can I honestly say I have given it time, study, and pursuit? Have I given myself a fair shake, or have I drifted and procrastinated?

(4) For those of us who claim religious adherence, just who has come first in our lives, the great I Am or God? Have we really accepted God?

(5) Am I willing to turn my life and will over to the care of God, as I understand Him?

b. *To Myself*
(1) Have I honestly faced myself or have I sidestepped through day dreaming, wishful thinking, resentments, self pity, and the bottle?

(2) Am I satisfied with myself, my responsibilities, morals disposition, the example I set, my family relations?

(3) Haven't I been cheated and short-changed through dishonesty to myself? How badly?

(4) A change of attitude to the old alibi: "I can't take this anymore" to, "I can take this and a lot more for this day."

c. *To My Family*
(1) Do I recall my marriage vows? Have I lived up to them? (Be careful, don't start taking your wife's inventory.)

(2) Have I gained and kept the love and respect of my children? Do I want them to be honorable, happy,

well adjusted? Has my training and example emphasized those aims? Has my drinking helped my children?

   (3) Do I dictate to my family, or have I created trust and
love through unselfishness, interest, and examples?

   (4) Do I want my children to turn out like me?

d. *To My Work*

   (1) "No matter what the job, do it well." Is that for others, or do I apply it to myself, as well?

   (2) Am I carrying my weight in my work or have I been a
50% man on the job due to my drinking? Am I producing or just getting by?

   (3) Has my relationship with my boss and fellow workers
(associates) been on an honest level, or has it been
filled with resentments, pettiness, deceit, and self pity?

   (4) Have I discharged my responsibilities well to my associates, clients, and others involved in my work?

   (5) Are there any ethical considerations in my work that
clash with my moral standards, or do I excuse it on
the basis that it is "business"?

   (6) Am I doing the kind of a job I would expect if someone was working for me?

e. *To My Friends, Neighbors, and Community*

   (1) Do I cultivate friends for what I can get out of them?
Does friendship have my price tag attached?

   (2) Frankly, am I interested in my neighbor, their kids,
the welfare of our churches, schools, and community
projects or don't I give a hoot?

   (3) Do I consider myself a worthy citizen of city and
country, or am I taking a free ride? Am I a respected
member of my community?

   (4) Does the Golden Rule apply in my relationships with
people, or is it me first, last, and always?

5. *Responsibilities*
    a. *To God*
        (1) The daily pursuit and daily practice of faith through proper prayer, meditation, and attitude.
        (2) Applying Step #3. Let go—let God.
        (3) Practicing the precepts of spirituality: reverence, love, charity, and moral responsibility.
        (4) Learning and exercising gratitude as one of the greatest of graces and the key to happiness.
        (5) Picking myself up when I fall.
        (6) Interest in the welfare of others.
        (7) Honoring God in His own home—the church of my choice—each Sunday.
    b. *To Myself*
        (1) To determine what I want in life and to seek the necessary help to realize it. Required: honesty, intellect, effort, time.
        (2) To become cognizant of my daily obligations, recognizing their fulfillment is essential to my peace of mind and sobriety.
        (3) To put First Things First, to accept what must be accepted, and never again to short change or deceive myself.
        (4) To look for the wonders and beauty in life, instead of facing the wrong direction.
        (5) A change of attitude to the old alibi! "I can't take this anymore" to "I can take this and a lot more for this day."
    c. *To My Family*
        (1) To cherish: they are mine and a part of me. They look to me for love, guidance, example, admonition, leadership, and spiritual and material care. Almighty God and I shape their destiny.
        (2) To love: Not only the self indulgent type, but more to

plan for, fight for, sacrifice for—to make them finer people.

(3) To provide: our families come first; we, second. Their needs, worries, interests come before ours. That's as it should be.

(4) To enjoy: family outings, family interests, shows together, games with the kids. Finally, praying together. Those are the cherished memories.

d. *To My Work*

(1) Above all, to seek balance. If I am lazy, to put more effort into the job and establish order; if I am unrealistic, to seek work in keeping with my capabilities; if I am gifted, to utilize those abilities, but never to the exclusion of spiritual, personal, and family obligations.

(2) To keep an eagle eye beamed on Money for Money's sake, power (position), and personal acclaim. They are the alcoholic's poison.

(3) To deal with people in my work as ethically as I do in any phase of living—if I want peace with myself.

(4) To be less demanding and more producing; business is always looking for the better man. Our rewards will come if we want them.

(5) Am I doing the kind of a job I would expect if someone was working for me?

e. *To AA*

(1) To always remember: "To God and AA, I owe my deliverance." My obligation is twofold—to be the best AA I can and to help make it available to others.

(2) My knowledge of alcoholism and AA, principles means nothing, unless applied constantly. One "must" to my continued sobriety is regular attendance at group meetings.

(3) My sobriety is contingent not on admittance, but acceptance and undertaking of all 12 Steps.

(4) To contribute to my group's betterment. If their idea of a meeting is a bragging contest on history making binges, suggest more solid material, such as one of the Steps. The caliber of the meeting is all important—to me and to each member.

(5) Be careful how you live. You may be the only copy of the Big Book other people ever read.

Fifth Step Lecture Transcription
REV. GORDON GRIMM

At this meeting, we are going to talk about Step Five, and hopefully from this meeting, you will have an understanding of what we expect out of you and also what you can expect out of us.

Step Five reads: "Admitted to God, to ourselves, and another human being, the exact nature of our wrongs." As many of you are well aware, these Steps in the AA program are not steps in isolation. What is involved in Step Five is very dependent on the previous Step Four. And that Step reads: "Took a searching and fearless moral inventory of ourselves." In essence, this is a therapeutic process. I'd like to point out that this is a process that was arrived at—five people in very desperate straits, and they found that they needed to do their own inventory, and then they needed to tell someone else about it. I don't think there's anything magical about a Fifth Step. In essence, I think it's a great deal of hard work. The essence is found in Paul Tournier's quotation when he wrote: "We only become fully aware of that about ourselves if we are willing to communicate it to another human being."

Now in your process of recovery at Hazelden, you are going to find that the clergy are the ones that are going to hear your Fifth Steps. They are the ones who are functioning as 'another human being.' A great deal of the thought that has gone into that decision is based on the fact that we have a lot of experience in hearing and accepting confidential material.

I'd like to share with you some of my own experiences, in particular the one that revolved around my own inventory and Fifth Step. I don't happen to be chemically dependent today, and I started in this business when I was a theological student at a seminary in St. Paul. In 1957 I was sent out to Willmar State

Hospital, where they had 270 beds for alcoholics. The treatment that developed at Willmar influenced what we do here at Hazelden. In 1957, I left my internship three times. One of the reasons was that the people who sat on the other side of the desk, who were identified as patients, I felt they were much more honest with themselves than I was able to be with myself at that time. Now the third time that I was going to leave my internship, Dr. Bradley, the psychiatrist in charge of the hospital, called me in and said, "Grimm, you have ten days in which to take an inventory. You have to tell me who heard your Fifth Step. And that's a condition for you to function on this staff."

Now, honestly, when I left the state hospital, which is about 103 miles west of the Twin Cities, I drove to Minneapolis, I was sure I would never return to Willmar. During that trip into Minneapolis, I kept on reviewing how the patients at the hospital were willing to face up to themselves. That really made an impression on me. Sometime during that trip, I decided that I would follow through with Dr. Bradley's suggestion.

I think that the two ingredients that probably keep most of us from facing up to ourselves are probably fear and pride. Many, many recovering people have informed me that they felt that the single most important process in their recovery was the process around the Fifth Step. That's what helped them face up to themselves. That is what helped them overcome their fear.

When I left Willmar State Hospital, I thought alcoholics had it easy, and the expectation that I take a Fourth and Fifth Step was asking a lot, if not too much, of me. Today we really believe that this process could benefit anybody. I can readily understand that some of you sitting here today believe that if you were not in a treatment center for alcoholism, maybe you wouldn't have to go through this process. There may be a great deal of truth in that. But we would like you to approach this in a manner that this is a real opportunity for you that others will not enjoy in their lifetime which is a loss for them. If you want to, think of all of the other kinds of problems that human be-ings can have, and they can still evade facing up to themselves. Your roommates, other members of your family, can benefit a great deal from this kind of process. But we expect that it is going to become a part of your recovery process here.

I'd like to point out a couple of issues. Number one, you may be asking yourself the question: What is significant about this process? Around here we're involved in a great deal of group therapy. What is really unique about Steps Four and Five?

When I went out to Willmar, I was involved also in a gradu-ate program in Group Psychology and for a year I had been par-ticipating on a weekly basis in groups. For me what is unique and distinct and different about the Fifth Step in relationship to group therapy is that in the Fifth Step, you have to own up to your own behavior—you have to say "this is me." If you think about it a little bit, it's a great deal different than quietly sitting in a group where other people around you point out observa-tions about you which you can passively acknowledge. Now I'm not going to publicly take my first Fifth Step with you, but I will share with you what was the most important thing for me.

I simply had no understanding or appreciation for the way in which my anger and hostility towards my father, who had been an alcoholic, was getting in my way. My father was treated three times in the state hospital in Iowa and lived the last nine years of his life sober. My parents separated after the third time my father had been treated. All that time, whenever I got into trouble, I said to myself, "What can you expect from the son of an alcoholic?"

Now what was different in my Fifth Step, I feel, was this: During the year of group therapy, any number of people pointed out to me my anger and hostility. And I acknowledged that. I ac-knowledged every bit of it. But it was in a passive sort of way, in a manner that I didn't have to own for myself. Now something happened in my Fifth Step—that 'fearless and searching' part of the inventory. I can't say that I was just totally conscious of the process, but taking the Fifth Step made a huge difference. I actively talked about and owned all of the anger, resentment, and hostility that I had kept inside myself.

This stuff went back long before group therapy. I had college and high school football coaches who pointed out that if somebody poked me in the nose, I was really a good defensive tackle. And I was. But I didn't see how that cancer inside me was interfering in my relationships. In taking the Fifth Step, I don't expect that you're going to learn a great deal new about yourselves. In the environment and program that we have designed here your peers get a pretty good handle on their perceptions of you. Now what is unique about your inventory and your Fifth Step is that you become the one who owns what you admit to yourself, in the presence of God, and another human being.

I want to say some things about the way in which you begin this process. I think it would be better that you begin as human beings. Don't start out as alcoholics or chemically dependent people. If you do that you're going to find that you are a part of what our whole culture believes today. Most of you, by the time you get here in treatment, feel you're second, third, or fourth-class citizens, or you wouldn't be alcoholics in the first place. Now that's the way our culture feels with this issue. You've got to get beyond that. You've got to start first as human beings who happen to have either the problem of alcoholism or chemical dependency. And that your task is to inventory yourself in such a manner so that you know what it is you want to talk about with the person who's going to hear your Fifth Step.

There are some great things about the treatment center and this environment. But sometimes we expect too much of the patients in terms of the things that they are expected to accomplish in a short period of time. But we're trying to do better. The Fifth Step process seems to mirror this. There is not enough effort and time to give positive affirmation to who you are as human beings. There isn't enough time devoted in the rehabilitation to identify positive human qualities and characteristics. It's our belief that if you leave here thinking that you're no damn good, you're not going to devote much effort or energy towards your own rehabilitation. If in the process you believe that you are worth the time, effort, and energy that it is going to take you, then you're going to be willing to take some time. You're going to be willing to expend some energy towards your own recovery.

Here, if you say a positive thing about yourself, you're accused of false pride. Now put some of that in perspective when you are going about your own inventory. It's going to be very, very important that you see yourself—the whole picture of yourself.

One other aspect. Since there are about 150 people present for this lecture this morning it is impossible to deal with the unique aspects of each one of you. Because of the educational dimension of the lectures, much of what we have to present to you is of a more general nature. We try desperately and very hard to apply the knowledge that we know about alcoholism and chemical dependency as it affects most people. Stay away from generalizations when you are dealing with your own inventory. Make your inventory and its content as specific as you can. Remember that as far as human lives go, uniqueness is not something worthless. It becomes priceless. In your recovery, if you are going to deal with yourself as human beings, you are going to have to come to some understanding of who you are as a unique human being, with the condition or disease of alcoholism or chemical dependency.

Remember that there's nothing magical about this. It's not going to be an easy process. Oftentimes, people who take their own inventory tend to isolate themselves and just stay in their room, getting depressed with what they find out about themselves. I'll never forget when I took my first Fifth Step with a theological professor who was very, very close to me. He had a soft smile on his face when I talked about the shame I felt, and the fear. That smile communicated a great deal to me. Now, if you see people on your unit that you know are working on their Fifth Step and they begin to isolate themselves, reach out a little bit and talk with them. It may happen to you, too, in your process. We're strange creatures, we human beings. If you find yourself in your process wanting to lock yourself in your room, getting a little depressed, that's the time to get out on your unit and talk with the other people who are living with you. I think you're going to discover some fascinating things about yourself and the others on your unit. You know, none of us has to live with anyone else in this world; it's not that kind of requirement.

One of the things about this unit concept at Hazelden is that you learn that your friends, whom you never knew before you got here, can see the positive qualities in you that you can't see in yourself. If you intend to be serious about your recovery then you have to listen to what some of your friends are saying. Many, many people have said to me that the most important thing about this process is not an earth shattering revelation about themselves but the simple fact that they can face themselves when they look in the mirror. And that they can be pleased and thankful to God that they were given life on this earth. That's a very different way than they had thought before.

Now enough about what we expect of you. I want to share with you what you have as a right to expect from us. Everyone here at Hazelden who hears Fifth Steps has gone through the same process—their own Fourth Step inventory, and their own Fifth Step. They have to know personally and experientially what these Steps are about. You are not used as guinea pigs. It's not that we believe that this is good for you and not good for us. This process is a human process. I want to share something with you about your Fourth Step Guide. There is no human defect discussed in any Fourth Step Guide I have ever seen that only applies to alcoholics or chemically dependent people. All of the defects apply to all human beings. That's what this process is about.

Now, while we as clergy are listening to another person's Fifth Step, I think it's very important that you realize that our goal is to be respectful at all times of your dignity. We try to do this in the way we become involved with you and in the way in which we listen to you.

Here is a list of questions of what the clergy person looks for in the Fifth Step. The first question: Does this person know what his or her task is with me? Let me translate that for you. It means: Has this person completed his or her own inventory? It's not the clergy's task to carry out your personal inventory. It is your task; it is your inventory. It is our task to get the total picture that you present and reflect it back to you as another human being. We don't just sit there like bumps on a log.

The second question: Is this person really seeing him or herself or are they self-deluded? Let me give you an example. I suppose if I were to give one phrase about the typical cultural attitude towards alcoholism, it would go something like this. An alcoholic is like Dr. Jekyll and Mr. Hyde. When drunk they are rotten. When sober they are wonderful. Now that is a superficial understanding. If you think that it's only the qualities that you have to deal with while you're drinking, you're still self-deluded. Some people have described alcoholics as being more like civil wars than human beings. The task of this process is to bring those two personality conflicts together so that you find a level of acceptance as human beings, both the dark side and the light side.

That's what question three is about: Is this person demonstrating some level of personal self-acceptance?

Number four: Has this person established priorities? Let me

give you my own first Fifth Step experience. I used an old, old guide that had thirteen personality defects in it. And when I finished telling Dr. Smits what I had to tell him about myself, he asked me what I was going to do. And I very positively pointed out all the thirteen areas I was going to work on. And he said, "My God, Grimm, your grandiosity is really showing. Most of us human beings can work on one issue at a time, not thirteen. If you are going to take thirteen, I think that's a guarantee that you're not going to work on any. If you have to pick one, I suggest this. Pick the defect that is most threatening to your recovery. That deserves your first, undivided attention." I have taken three Fifth Steps since 1957; I have not found that I have less defects to deal with. I don't want to mislead you. This process is not going to make angels out of human beings. For me, if this process leads in any direction, the Twelve Steps lead downward to humility, not upward to some kind of perfection. You are not going to become better human beings by doing a Fifth Step. You're going to become different human beings. You're going to deal in a different way with yourself and those around you.

That's what the fifth question has to deal with: Are you willing to change? Bottom line is change in this business. Are you willing to make some modifications?

I have to add a number six because so many times for a week after this lecture, people will come up to me in the hallway and say, "Chaplain Grimm, that was a nice lecture but . . . ." About a month ago, a fellow came up to me whom I knew for a long time, lives in the community I live in, and he said, "That was all very good. I have twenty-seven pages of defects. And the positive qualities I know about myself I can write on the inside of a matchbook. Now something is out of whack." And I just had to tell him, "You haven't spent enough time on assessing your positive qualities." And he went back to the unit where everybody else could give him a whole list, but he couldn't. We want you to be able in a positive way to talk about your positive qualities. To own them as much as you're going to own your negative qualities and your defects.

I want to close with another quotation from Paul Tournier, because this for me is the essence of the Fifth Step process. "You have come to a crossroads. I have no doubt that God has brought you to this present moment. There are two roads in front of you. One goes clinic to clinic. It is full of suffering, but it is relatively easy to take. This is the road along which you expect healing to come from others, from doctors clever enough to discover some new remedy, which will cure you. The second is much harder. If you take it, you must accept what comes to you, clear your thoughts, put up with your troubles, have the courage to go back to work, and face up to life even though it hurts. This is the road, which demands a change of heart. But most who travel this road do not travel it alone. And even if it demands the greatest of sacrifices, most who travel this find great joy in it because as they travel this road, they find many of their friends. And most find that this is the road that their God also travels."

About the Author

DAMIAN MCELRATH, PH.D., has served in a variety of positions at Hazelden from 1977 until his retirement in 1995, most notably as executive vice president of Recovery Services. McElrath came to Hazelden after twenty years of teaching, counseling, and administrative work; he was president of St. Bonaventure University from 1972 to 1976. He is well known for his lectures on addiction, spirituality, and the Twelve Steps and lectured at the Rutgers Summer School of Alcohol Studies and its European branch from 1980 to 2001. He has published numerous scholarly books and articles on historical and theological topics and is the author of the Hazelden books *Patrick Butler: A Biography, Dan Anderson: A Biography, Hazelden: A Spiritual Odyssey,* and *Further Reflections on Hazelden's Spiritual Odyssey.*